Between the Rock of Marriage and the Hard Place of Separating

A Practical Guide and Personal Experience

by

Gilli Stephens

ISBN-13: 978-1512312263

ISBN-10: 1512312266

DEDICATION

For my three beloved children, Charlotte, Benedict and Rosamund.

For my mother who reared me with her love, her wit, her wisdom, Sufi philosophies, and is the one who said, "This is the most extraordinary separation I have ever heard of; write a book."

For my sisters, Jane and Sally.

For Robert.

For my many supportive, fair and impartial friends.

For Frances Grant for her editing skills, patience and loving support.

For Dr K Bradford Brown and Roy Whitten, co-founders of the Life Training Programme now called More to Life, creators of experiential self-development courses without which I would not have come this far. I continue to draw on the many insights, nuggets and wisdoms I have learned in the thirty years of participating and teaching this work.

My thanks to you all for your upholding and honouring of me, however stuck I have been!

CONTENTS

ACKNOWLEDGMENTS

All quotations by Drs Jordan & Margaret Paul © Jordan Paul & Margaret Paul published by Haxelden Foundation.

All quotations by George Bach & Ronald Deutsch © George R. Bach & Ronald M Deutsch published by Berkley Books.

All quotations by K Bradford Brown © K Bradford Brown, published by Life Times Press.

All quotations by John Gottman © John Gottman, published by Bloomsbury Publishing plc.

All quotations by Wayne Dyer M.D. © Dr Wayne Dyer, published by Hay House, Inc.

All quotations by Louise Hay © Louise L. Hay, published by Hay House Inc.

I would like to emphasise that this guide gives my impressions of the law in UK and is not definitive. Please take legal advice before acting on any suggestions given here.

Foreword

I offer this guide to you, the reader.

Maybe you have picked up this book because you want to leave your partner, have been left, or want to pass it on to a friend in need.

I have been here, and I was so totally lost I want to save you some of the pitfalls, pinch-points and pain. This is not a book full of legal information; you can get that from lawyers, solicitors and citizen advice bureaus. Nor does it set out intending that you will reconcile; there are plenty of organizations, counsellors, books and well-meaning friends to help you. Nor is it the ins and outs of the D- word, which I could not even say.

It is, however, written for those of you who are afraid, angry, resentful and in pain. It is for those of you still pretending to the outside world that you are happy but secretly looking for a way out, who may be reading this down the bed with a torch. It is for those of you who have been left and are now swept up in a procedure you do not want, cannot fathom and from which you are hurting through and through.

This book is so designed that each chapter stands alone, in order that you can dip into the book on any topic – or you can read it straight through. It is all relevant. It is my best shot at giving you an emotional road map, a manual to help.

Whatever the outcome I wish you well, and good luck with the rest of your life – which starts today.

Gilli Stephens, 2014

1. Hope versus Fear

'Lose money, lose little. Lose pride, lose much. Lose hope, lose all.'

- Anon

As a couple we do not just suddenly arrive at separation or termination of our relationships. Instead we *think* about it, often long and hard. We may go through years of happiness interspersed with phases of deterioration.

These phases occur long before legal separation. I call it 'uncoupling', therapists call it emotional divorce.

On the surface you still appear together in every way but inside that special connection has died. Once this has happened I believe we go into that stagnant stage of 'existing' together and this can drag out for years. Once this stage becomes the norm of the partnership it is extremely difficult to reverse it especially if it is neither discussed nor recognized nor dealt with.

So when emotional divorce has already happened why do we continue to stay in the relationship? I believe we stay out of hope or fear.

Hope

Hope is incredibly sustaining. Hope comes with courage, it comes with trust, it comes with beliefs, and it comes with faith.

But are you still in your relationship *only* out of hope – hope that it will change, hope that it will get better, hope the other will give up their infidelity, hope that you will conceive a child, hope that this is a passing stage, and hope that all will be well soon?

Without hope we would be a sorry species, for hope keeps us alive. It is, however, both a strength and a weakness. Jonathan Cainer of the *Daily Mail* says, "Hope can give us strength, yet it can also cause us to be weak. When we hold on to a reasonable hope, we find courage to proceed through difficult territory. When we hold onto unreasonable, far-fetched or wildly optimistic hope, we can end up dwelling far too long in a place we ought to leave."

Let us take this wisdom sentence by sentence. Maybe hope has been sustaining you for some time. It has made you strong to cope, it has given you enough to have you remain and try to improve the situation.

***

> **Hope can make you strong enough to cope, and therefore remain and try to improve the situation**

Or perhaps, instead, it has made you weak, and you are now in a victim role of 'poor me' which is unlikely to make your partner want to stay. Unfortunately, when we dread something – a partner leaving, for instance – we start to do things in order to make them stay. Feeling powerless and unhappy, we play games, and although these are unlikely to be new behaviours they do take on an exaggerated role as we try to control the situation.

The more we try and control, the more the other will pull away, and in the end we get what we dread - the departure of the beloved. In fact this behaviour may literally have driven the other away when it was your intention to keep them.

Thus, having hope (because you think you are in control of the situation) turns out to be a weakness.

***

> **The more we try and control, the more the other will pull away, and in the end we get what we dread – the departure of the beloved**

Holding a reasonable hope of reconciliation, it is true that you will find the courage to hang in there through difficult, turbulent and miserable times. If you have bought this book because you are toying with the idea of separating you will know if your hope is well founded and you have something to save.

If, on the other hand, you have bought this book because you have reached the stage of 'wildly optimistic hope' that anything can be salvaged, it may well be time to move on before all vestiges of decency, respect and dignity shrivel up.

Fear

I believe fear is the other basis for remaining in a relationship. If you dispute this, ask yourself, why are you still there? What are you afraid of?

Let's look at some categories which might produce fear: emotional issues, physical and verbal bullying, lack of romance, and financial concerns.

Emotions

Do you believe that there will be no-one else to love you? No-one to care for you and no-one to take care of? i.e. 'I am not needed.' Are you afraid of being alone?

Alternatively, it could be that your self-esteem needs to have a partner physically on your arm and in your bed in order to send the signal, 'I have someone, so I am OK.'

Physical and verbal bullying

Are you afraid of being hit physically? What about verbal bullying and threats which are as frightening as being actually hit? It is the sense of powerlessness, and the fear of reprisal that has us stay.

Romance

Are you caught in the fear of lack of romance in your life? Do you in fact have any romance in a miserable relationship? Are you kidding yourself that romance lasts? How disillusioned are you that romance did not endure into a lasting love? Are you telling yourself that anything is better than nothing –

so you stay?

Finance

If you lose your partner will you lack security? How will you finance yourself (and your children) on your own? The fear may be, 'I can't cope, I've never earned enough to survive on my own, I'll be sleeping on a park bench.' If you are unhappy but have absolute financial security and backing then I believe the reason you have remained is out of hope.

Either way, however, there is one hope I would encourage you to *not* to give up: the hope that whatever the outcome you will remain talking, reasonable, sane, caring human beings who once loved each other enough to agree 'till death do us part' if you married.

It is not the object of this book to delve into what went wrong. There are a lot of books and courses and therapists to help you to do that. Nor is the object to point fingers, blame or judge.

***

The object of this book is to guide you through all the different aspects that you will need to make decisions about if you tread the separation path.

Perhaps you will not get that far and this book will lie redundant at the back of your bookcase. Perhaps, after trying the processes in both the communications chapter and the resentment chapter, you will have a new understanding of each other so you are going forward together with renewed hope.

At all times I urge you to take responsibility for how you use this book. It is not a weapon to threaten your partner with. Instead it is an aid, guide, and manual to help you give it your best shot to part on terms which will honour and respect and even love this other human being to whom you once meant so much and who once meant so much to you.

2. Fantasy versus Reality

We all have fantasies. What's yours? Did you begin your partnership with a fantasy of marriage? Did you grow up with an ideal picture of how it would be? Are you programmed with society's suggestions, habits, and culture or with your family's role model, beliefs and ideals?

We each of us have absorbed and either accepted or rejected the ideals around us. Perhaps you grew up in a home which you want to emulate… or, in no circumstances will you let your homes be the same as that one! As children we learn to comply or defy authority and as adults we do just the same, and in addition we justify doing so.

***

As children we learn to comply or defy authority.

What was, or is, your fantasy of a relationship? What did you dream of? What have you worked for? What was your desire? Your expectations versus your present reality?

You are reading this book because you are

thinking of separating. Things are not going according to the dream.

In a relationship you will be surrounded by negative tendencies to be adjusted to and overcome by both of you – being critical, negative, deferring to, self-righteous, too judgmental, impatient, intolerant and so on. This is not what you had expected; somehow your joy is turning to disillusionment. Now is when we try to change the other. Now is when our own faults get overlooked because we can only notice those in our partner. Our own behaviour and our own negativity have now become OK and worse, we believe we are the one who is *right*.

So what is the reality here? Is it just that you need to adjust a bit or are you seriously incompatible? John Gray says, "Physical chemistry generates desire and arousal. Emotional chemistry generates affection, caring and trust. Mental chemistry creates interest and receptivity. Spiritual chemistry opens our hearts, creating love, appreciation and respect." Do you have all four going for you? Which one has faded? Which one is your desert? Which one remains?

It is not essential to have all four to make a lasting relationship because we find coping mechanisms to deal with what is missing. For instance, if you do not have many interests in common your mental stimulus may come from taking up and pursuing your own interests, you may even go back to university. For spiritual comfort you may get involved with a church or other spiritual outlet for yourself. Sadly, I think a physical desert in your life will result in an affair.

This leaves 'emotions generating affection'.

My research shows that many marriages jog along in this capacity. There is enough affection to stay, enough hope that things will change, enough friendship to think that 'This will do,' or enough fantasy remaining to go on trying.

Have you stayed together too long?

John Gray also says, "One of the reasons people end relationships with negative feelings is that they stay together too long. They do not recognise they are with the wrong person and move on. Instead, they try too hard to make a relationship work. They either try to change their partner or try to change themselves. In the process of trying to fit together, they make things worse. In trying to make a relationship that is close to the right one *into* the right one, they create frustration and disappointment. In the process of trying to make things better, they bring out the worst in their partner and themselves."

In other words, trying to fulfil the fantasy of this being the 'right one', are you in fact ignoring the reality that this is not the person for you? In trying to make a relationship more than it is, trying to fit when there is no fit, are you giving yourself and those around you unnecessary pain and strife? Maybe your reality is that it is time to move on.

***

In trying to fulfil the fantasy of this person being the 'right one', are you in fact ignoring the reality that this is not the person for you?

Letting go

This phrase is easily said and can be so hard to do. You have history, nostalgia and maybe children together. Well-meaning friends will encourage you, distract you and even float new mates past you – all to no avail if you have not let go.

Nothing anyone said or did for me helped until I looked squarely at the fantasy I was still hanging onto. My friend Jo said to me, "Gilli, you chased a fantasy of marriage while you were in the marriage, it's why you kept trying, but did you get it with him? The reality is no, so why are you still holding a fantasy about him outside of the marriage?" At last it penetrated; my fantasy did not match my reality *with him*.

***

> **Does your fantasy match your reality with this particular partner?**

This is not to say that all fantasies are unobtainable. I think they can be realized, but probably with someone else. The point is to recognise when it is not a fit with this particular person, and therefore to let go.

3. Marriage versus Relationship

One of the most important comments a friend made to me was, "You sound like you want the marriage but not the relationship."

I had not seen it like this before. It was true, I was miserable in the relationship but I wanted to be married. I had not thought to separate these two components in this way.

I believe that if you want both, and the relationship is working, then you have a happy marriage. Indeed, mine had been this way for many years. However, over thirty-three years there are growth areas, changes, adjustments and different passages of age. If this takes place for one and not the other, or if the time lag for catching each other up is too long, then disharmony creeps in and eventually prevails.

***

> *Over time, disharmony creeps in when personal growth takes place for one but not the other.*

You then have the choice: will you muddle along as you have been? What is your particular muddle?

Are you blaming your spouse without looking at your behaviour? Are you constantly pleasing, doing anything to keep the peace? Will you remain in the relationship as a martyr and tyrant to those around you? Will you have an affair and believe you are happier? Will you wait for your other half to have the affair and then you can justify throwing them out or going yourself? Would you rather be together warts and all rather than not at all? Or has it got so bad you would rather be on your own?

I had a lot of fears about being on my own. Did I even like being on my own? I believed I did not, since I do not even like walking a dog alone! I like company. I like people.

Also, how would I survive financially? I married at nineteen and been a 'kept woman' ever since. My money-earning capabilities had been confined to hobbies doing well. Now I would be out in the job market, wishing to live in the style to which I had become accustomed, only to find myself unemployable next to bright young things with a degree. I was very, very scared, and without a doubt stayed in the relationship in order to be married and secure, for longer than I needed.

So, marriage spelt security to me, socially and financially. The institution of marriage gave me status, meaning: I was a Mrs, a wife and mother, my childhood dream. Did I really want to let go of all that and maybe be associated with the D—word? I now know how many women are still in marriages for the same reason.

Being reassured and told over and over again that I would be OK, that I was a survivor, that I would make a living, simply did not penetrate; it certainly did not enable me to act.

So what did help me? Mulling over this difference between marriage and the relationship a friend came up with an idea.

"Every time," she said, "that you behave or react as Mrs Stephens, I will let you know. Likewise, every time you are being authentically Gilli, I will let you know." She did. And it was this flag for me that had me notice just how often my role as Mrs Stephens clashed with how I wanted to be as me, Gilli.

Ultimately I began to be braver about living as Gilli. And as I got braver I could see that the route ahead was to leave. This was still terrifying so my halfway house was to take a flat for an agreed time. My bewildered husband agreed to this separation, agreed to pay for the flat and even agreed to take his turn out of our joint house – possibly because at that stage he hoped I'd get over my aberration, be lonely and bolt home.

Living in my little rented flat, alone for the first time in thirty-three years, I was in heaven. I knew very quickly that I loved my freedom, that I would survive and that I would create an income somehow. Suddenly it was no longer scary, it was now possible; I could attain this joy for the rest of my life! However, at times this knowledge would disappear, and nostalgia, history and love of my family would tug – and still I could not make the break.

So my husband and I swapped places. I went back home and he moved to the little flat. I had fears that because I was back in my familiar surroundings and environment that my newfound strength as Gilli would evaporate and I would slip back into Mrs Stephens. This did happen when he came round. It was hard on home turf not to play familiar games and roles, particularly, it seemed, for my husband, who was understandably resentful at not being in his home when he did not want this separation in the first place.

***

> **Your new found strength can evaporate when confronted with the familiar games and roles played by your partner.**

I decided I wanted to make the separation permanent, but still I could not find my voice to say it. It seemed so final, such a waste of thirty-three years, such sadness to me not to have lived out my marriage vows. Couldn't I just keep going? No I could not. And I finally found my voice over a misunderstanding that had me get angry enough for it to finally come out of my mouth. Not the best way to drop this bombshell. As a result my husband thought I did not mean it, and that I had just said it out of anger and pique. We limped on, me mentally dividing our possessions, he in disbelief. At last his sister came to stay and reported back to him that I meant it.

The stages of loss and grief

Dr Elizabeth Kubler-Ross was one of the first to acknowledge the existence of five stages in the loss process and to give them names. She repeatedly saw these stages either in her dying patients themselves or with their families. What is now clear is that we go through these same stages, in various strengths, whether we have lost the car keys, moved house, divorced or are confronted with death.

Thus, if your partner has announced they love another and want to separate, or if you have been plotting and planning and wanting to leave for years, you will still go through the same loss stages.

· DENIAL and SHOCK - Denial is a defence – a normal, healthy way of coping with horrible news, often unexpected, and sometimes sudden or bad news.

· RAGE and ANGER - When denial is no longer feasible it is replaced by anger. This stage is especially difficult for families and friends, etc. The hurt person's anger scatters like buckshot. Fragments fly in every direction. It hits everyone. This anger should not be taken personally.

· BARGAINING - This is seen in those quickie prayers we make to God. Sometimes we raise the ante to absurd levels in our effort to change the outcome.

· DEPRESSION - This arises from the changes taking place. It results from believing that you are losing everything and everyone you love. In this state, there is no bright side. Nor are there any soothing words that can be said to alleviate the state of mind that has given up on the past and cannot fathom the unfathomable future.

· ACCEPTANCE - This is the final stage. You may not be happy but you will no longer be depressed or angry. Your acceptance may also be resignation to the fact that it has happened or will happen.

(Extract from *The Wheel of Life* by Elizabeth Kubler-Ross)

 Personal experience

I would recommend you learn to recognize these stages both in yourself and your partner. I bounced around them and they were not in order; maybe this was because I was instigating the changes, I was leaving. I did notice my husband very clearly in each stage and I found myself more tolerant because I understood.

Shock

A word about shock: people can and do say some very odd things in shock. The brain, frantically looking for something familiar to hang on to, will come out with anything. A friend of mine after another night-time row found the courage to leave then and there. She also found herself standing in the kitchen at 2.00 a.m. opening cupboards and wondering if she should take the crisp packets with her! Similarly, when I told my husband I wanted to separate, his very first sentence was, "How will I get my *Lands' End* catalogue?"

***

> **While functioning in shock people can and do say
> some very odd things.**

Do not take what he/she does or says as something personal or as a weapon to be used. At no time do I tell myself that if that is all my husband could say it shows he never loved me. This would not be true. Functioning in shock is robotic and I beg you to make allowances for whatever takes place at that time.

4. Separation versus Divorce?

I thought that separation was a nice comfortable word to use. It was a state of being which I could try, and there was a way back. I had no idea that it actually means something different in the law – that, once embarked on, the law will refer back everything to the date you stopped cohabiting, *not* when you decide to make it permanent, *not* when you find a convenient date for tax reasons, *not* a different date because your partner never really believed you meant it. The law takes the date either when one of you moved out or when circumstances in the home indicate that you have separated.

***

The law takes the date either when one of you moved out or when circumstances in the home indicate that you have separated.

So what does separation mean versus a divorce?

There is a distinction between separation and divorce for financial settlement; the money valuation is dealt with differently. A separation agreement is generally treated as if moving towards a divorce and can be used in a divorce settlement.

Separation ensures you keep any gift given to you in name or bought with your own money. You keep anything you brought to the marriage including any inheritance you have received. However, pensions remain with and belong to the individual. A capital division of assets is taken from the date of separation but any resources you have now are taken into account.

There is a duty to support each other in separation, thus taking into account the earning capacities of each. Remember, although separated you are still technically 'married' so the wage earner is still obligated to support their partner.

Principles of fairness

You are entitled to a fair division of property including pensions but excluding gifts and inheritance. Amongst other circumstances that can be looked at will be:

· Cost of care of children

· Fair account of any economic advantage or economic disadvantage suffered by one party for the other unless they balance out

· Dependence of one party on the other to a substantial degree; a dependent is given up to three years to adjust

· Severe financial hardship

Ongoing periodical payments are called aliment, and periodical payment is called periodical allowance after divorce. Aliment is given on basis of different rules from periodical allowance.

Divorce aims to give a fair division of matrimonial property from the date of marriage to the date of separation; this includes pensions but excludes gifts and inheritances. If net capital is available at separation you have a right to a fair division. Any right to estate terminates on death of partner, unless agreed prior to divorce that there will be a capital sum on demise (see the chapter 'Your Will').

Your choices

Going for a clean break or receiving an allowance. It is important that you both know and understand the constraints of parting.

Rules of parting

· You may divorce if the marriage has irretrievably broken down because of adultery, desertion or unreasonable behaviour.

· You may divorce after two years with consent.

· You may divorce after five years without consent (usually).

It is also important to know the rules of your particular pension scheme, as this may influence and restrict your choices.

There is more on some of these topics in the

Money chapter.

Taking the final step

'In marriage we become partners for life in more ways than one. Those invisible bonds are seldom severed for any reason, including divorce.'

-K Bradford Brown

If your separation has been set up legally then if and when you come to divorce all should go through smoothly - you can even do it yourself.

Should you want to go ahead without a lawyer here are the steps:

Visit the website www.divorce-forms.co.uk for the appropriate form.

Ask for a divorce petition to be sent to you. In Scotland, call your local County Court for the petition.

1. Fill in the booklet (guidelines and examples are given) and sign it, which you as the Petitioner will do first. Post it to your partner, called the Respondent, who then signs their consent. It should be posted back to you for you to sign the affidavit and then lodge it with the court.

2. If the Respondent is resident in the UK they are given a week to return it. If they live abroad they are given six weeks.

3. You will need to include your marriage

certificate. A photocopy will not suffice for the Court. (After all, the Court cannot divorce you without proof of a marriage.) If yours is lost you can obtain another from the Register of Marriages from the town where the marriage was originally registered. You will need to supply both names, date and place, and enclose an SAE.

4. Now the machinations of the court grind away. After some weeks, the court will contact the Respondent and ask them if they still consent. At this point your partner can change their mind and say 'no'.

5. If the Respondent agrees (again six weeks if they live abroad) the court will grant the decree nisi.

6. After six weeks you can apply for the decree nisi to become absolute.

Note

If you are wanting to divorce before your two years separation is up you will have to decide which of the reasons for irretrievable breakdown you are going to agree to. Whichever you choose you will have to describe it in the space provided in the booklet.

If you have children you will be required to fill in a Statement of Arrangements form.

Your partner is given two opportunities to withhold consent.

You can consult a solicitor at any time but this will incur a cost.

5. Mediation versus Lawyers' Fees

Whether you plan to do the leaving, have left already, or have been left, you are going to need professional help. If you are speaking to each other, do consider Mediation as a quick, professional, cheap alternative to get you both to a point where your personal lawyer need only finalize the terms you have agreed.

As a couple we heard about CALM – Comprehensive Accredited Lawyer Mediators – and decided to find out more. Not all legal practices partake in this scheme, so it took some ringing around to find out who belonged to CALM in Scotland.

Alternatively, contact the Law Society and ask for Accredited Family Mediators in your area.

So what is the benefit of Mediation?

- You are in control
- You decide – not the courts
- It is less argumentative
- It is more informal, thus it saves you time, stress, and money, and is therefore better for you and any

children you have.

I suggest you consider Mediation by a lawyer who is an accredited Family Mediator if:

· You and your partner have separated or you are thinking about it.

· You would like to make arrangements in the best interests of any children involved.

· You want to work out what happens to the house.

Agreeing other financial issues

You want to do this together and as co-operatively as possible.

What mediation is

Mediation aims to help couples who are separating to consider the various options which may be available, and to help work out mutually acceptable arrangements. It helps you take into account the needs and feelings of any children who may be affected by the separation and its consequences.

The Mediator is neutral and impartial and helps individuals make appropriate decisions. The Mediator does not make decisions for you.

Why have a lawyer as a Mediator?

Lawyer Mediators are trained to deal with all issues

arising out of a separation, including child-related and financial.

A lawyer Mediator will help you gather all the information required to sort out the financial issues.

A lawyer Mediator is able to give you information about the legal framework and will assist you to identify a mutually acceptable formula for the resolution of all matters arising out of the separation.

Do I still need a Lawyer of my own?

Usually you will want the proposals, which your Mediator will summarize, incorporated into a binding agreement or Court Order by your own solicitor.

Is Mediation more expensive than going to court or solicitors in the first place?

No, it should be cheaper. Using Mediation to do the negotiations means that you and your partner share the cost of the Mediator instead of each paying separate solicitors for that stage.

How is Mediation paid for?

There is an hourly rate which you and your partner will share in whatever proportions you agree.

Does my partner have to agree to Mediation?

Yes, you have to attend Mediation sessions together. This may seem daunting but it is usually helpful in a general way to be able to sit down together on neutral territory with a Mediator. This is especially helpful to any children involved.

(Extract taken from CALM brochure)

Using a lawyer

If you choose to go the lawyer route, or you have to because your partner will not contemplate Mediation, I suggest you do the following:

· Ask your friends who have been through separation/divorce for their recommendations.

· Do not go to that friend of the family who happens to be a lawyer.

· Do pick the best person for the job *for you*, someone you like and trust and who does not have you believe you are stupid and incompetent, preferably a family divorce lawyer. There is no point going to a company or tax lawyer because he is a friend. You need someone rooting for you who is tip-top, especially if the going gets rough.

Friends have many horror stories about the fees of lawyers, and some can be expensive. Remember the length of every phone call is logged and every letter charged for. The more you can do with your partner, or on your own, the less you will be paying for the lawyer's time.

Personal experience

I found the lawyer I wanted and then informed him I was thinking of separating. He said he would wait to hear from me. I found this very comforting to know that at any time I could start the ball rolling and know I instantly had someone I trusted on my side.

When I did actually leave home, my husband and I created a consensual agreement, meaning that neither of our rights about the home, money, etc. was prejudiced. Faxing this to my lawyer for his advice was my first 'work' contact with him.

Thereafter we went to Mediation. How lucky we were to find this impartial, gentle, caring man. He was witness to some appalling behaviours, tears, arguments, fears and resentments. I do not know if he had had counselling training but he listened and gave out tissues like a pro! At all times he asked if both parties understood, and would patiently explain if we didn't. I was always heard and my views considered. I recommend this route.

When you have gone as far as you can go with the Mediator he will prepare a written summary, setting out the terms of any proposals resulting from the mediation. Then you will be encouraged to consult your independent solicitor advising you individually, who may then use the mediation summary as a basis for a legally binding settlement. The summary may lead to the submission of an application to a court for an order made at your joint request reflecting the terms of the summary.

Thus, you have saved time and money to get this far. For us it was then a matter of fine-tuning with our lawyers before we each signed.

Fees

We agreed we would each pay our lawyers ourselves but that my husband would cover the Mediation fees. This made sense as I still only had the house-keeping, which he gave me anyway, to draw from. Mediation tends to require three to eight sessions, lasting about one and half hours each.

There is no doubt that once in the lawyer's hands we had a period of going backwards as the two of them got picky about things we had already agreed. Luckily we both saw what was happening and instructed them to get on with how we had decided.

If you are not in communication with your partner except through the lawyers, it might be a good idea to have indicated your budget to your lawyer before embarking on problem-solving – which has a habit of becoming lengthy to your cost. Most lawyers can reduce their own legalese language!

I do not know what my husband paid his lawyer as he also had consultations about various tax implications.

6. Children, Family and Friends

Children

· Children want their parents together.

· If you have children, whatever their ages, they matter.

· Whatever their ages they will undoubtedly go through the five stages of loss (see the chapter 'Marriage versus Relationship').

· If they are little, do not think they automatically want to go along with your decisions.

· If they are big do not assume they will be adult and understanding.

Some pointers

Unless you have an Oscar in acting, do not think your children have not noticed the atmosphere, unhappiness, tears, silences, rows, etc. They will have. Children rarely confront you with what they have noticed, so nothing may be said but it will manifest in their behaviour.

Do not 'share' your troubles with them 'whatever their age'. Children are very protective of both of you, and criticizing the other's behaviour does not work. If they are little they may believe they have to choose between you, and if they are big they do not want their experience of the other parent spoiled. Traits that wind you up may be viewed by them as 'that's just Dad/Mum', and they may not share your opinion at all.

If it turns out that your split results in no communication between you both, do not ply the child with questions after a visit. If they return from a happy time to face an inquisition of questions they are likely to clam up, go silent, and be resentful of you. If they know they are returning to a parent who is pleased for them to have been with Mum/Dad, their story will come tumbling out. You may have to listen to eulogies about a new partner. Bite your tongue before you comment. Do your best to make your children's visits between you, the parents, open and loving. It will pay off. If your split results in open communication between you, and the children know and see this, they will then feel free to talk openly about each parent's visit. You will have gained.

***

**Do your best to make your children's visits
between you, the parents, open and loving**

Others' experience

How your children will behave over your separation will be unique to your family. However, since mine were older I thought it prudent to share the experiences of two friends who separated when their children were toddlers and teenagers. What happened and what to watch out for:

Helen's experience with daughters aged 5 years and 18 months

Helen had given her husband an ultimatum: choose between having affairs or the marriage. There was no response until the family had sold their home and were getting ready to move house when her husband walked in and said that he would not be moving with them.

Nearer to moving Helen told her oldest Jen, aged five, that their Daddy would not be moving with them but that she would have a special day with him each week. Tricia, the younger, aged eighteen months, went along so they had the visit together. Both children looked forward to it.

Even with the upheaval of moving nothing manifested in the children's behaviour until six months later. Unbeknownst to Helen, her husband was giving her six months to really miss him and find out how tough it was on her own; he fully expected her to ask him to get back together.

The husband, confident that Helen would return (even though he had left her) arrived at the house unexpectedly. An estate agent had called to collect some papers so, finding a man in the house, her husband misread the situation. An appalling row ensued. The upshot of this was that the husband started to make plans about taking the children away. Without telling Helen these plans, he used his visits to terrify the children about their security. He told them it was their secret that Daddy would collect them from school one day, no-one would know, and they'd go to France and live with their Granny and never see Mummy again because she was a bad woman.

Unable to tell Mummy because that would be breaking 'our secret' with Daddy, the frightened Jen started vomiting, refused to go to school and would get frequent bouts of diarrhoea. Eventually she did tell the story and Helen was able to reassure her that she would never be abandoned by Mummy. Helen told Jen that her Daddy was sick and not thinking properly. The child was instantly okay but she got very uptight over the next few months from not seeing her Daddy; it was six months before Helen allowed him to visit again.

Six years on, Tricia, the younger, is vehemently supportive of her father but secretly frightened of him. She refuses to accept anything her stepfather provides for her, including his love. She shuts down on him because she knows he's doing what a daddy should do but he's not her daddy. She constantly asks to know the truth about what happened. Both parents are giving her different stories.

Jen still adores her father and is also very afraid of him. She doesn't want to know what happened and prefers to avoid the truth. She treats her stepfather with disrespect and has learnt to use him when she needs him.

Helen believes that if it all happened now they would still be together. With the help available and her own self-development work, she would now seek other ways than leaving to address the problems in her marriage. Her deep regret is that she has repeated her own family experience of having no father present, with the result that her children, like she before them, no longer believe that they 'matter' to him.

Summary

Children do not comprehend the full situation like you do. Without certain knowledge they cannot understand why visits from a parent have stopped or changed, and they may harbour resentment towards you – when in fact you are doing your best to protect them.

Even if you, the adult, can see that the children are distressed, be careful of what you do, what you say and how you change the access.

***

Never ever be disrespectful, either about your ex-partner or to your ex- partner in front of your joint children.

Meg's experience with children aged 13, 9 and 6 years

In March, after being away for three weeks with her job Meg returned home and within two hours her husband told her he was leaving and she was not to try and stop him. They went to counselling where he said that he didn't want to leave and that he would give up the other woman. In August they had a lovely family holiday together but in September, on Ruth's seventh birthday, something made Meg ask if he was still seeing the other woman. When he said yes, she went into complete trauma, shock and rage, threw a plate at him and pushed him out of the front door.

The next day he returned, and sat down with Meg and the children and told them that he would be leaving because "*We* didn't want to live together." The children had no indication of what was coming, no clue to the pending change in their lives. Their happy life was gone in one sentence. Meg, aching with the deception of it all, was speechless at the use of the word 'we'. It was not what she wanted.

Meg, unable to accept her husband's lack of consideration and concern, became a defensive victim. Feeling impotent and powerless, she slipped into a huge hole, grabbing at anything to get out of it, which was mostly bitterness and hostility. With her in pieces and unable to function, the effect on the children was catastrophic.

Sarah, at thirteen years, developed ME most likely from the trauma of destabilisation of her family and her father's apparent lack of emotion about it. Benjamin, at nine years, went off the rails at school and was frequently sent home crying and distressed. He lost concentration and inner confidence. Ruth, at seven years, wanted everyone to be happy, didn't want to cause trouble and suffered in order not to 'bother Mummy'.

Ten years on Sarah still does not stand stress well. She tries to control a situation and when that does not work, becomes ill. Her father, who would never ever discuss it with her, seems to avoid being alone with her and then can only talk to her of trivial things. Although loving, Sarah believes she does not have a central place in her father's heart because she was the only child he did not have a bedroom for in his new flat. She refused to go to his wedding and changed her name to her mother's maiden name.

Benjamin put no effort into his time at school and did not pass any exams. He has the potential to be depressed and is the most angry of the three children. His friends are his pivot, not his family, and he puts energy and bonding into friendships. Ben's father remarried, had a baby son and converted Ben's room into the nursery without asking him. This displacement as son of the family made Ben furious. At nineteen he is just beginning to find an interest in life.

Ruth, now sixteen, still doesn't make any demands. Independent and the most shrewd of the three, she has the best relationship with her father because she doesn't ask him for answers.

Introducing a partner and a new baby

Sarah has never liked her father's new wife and refused to go to the wedding. Also, the fact that their flat did not have a bedroom for Sarah reinforced her belief that he didn't know how to cope with her negative reaction to his new wife.

Benjamin hated going to stay with his father and wife. Once, when Meg went on a long business trip, Ben had to stay there for a month. When Meg returned Ben shut himself in the bedroom for a week and was obviously deeply upset.

Ruth didn't know who to please. When the new wife dropped her off at school Meg would get upset. It was not an option for Ruth not to go and stay with Daddy.

When a new baby was on the way all three children were horrified. Their Dad's love was meagre enough and they did not want to share it. They cut him out. Of course the baby boy was loved on arrival but none of them gave him a present until he was five years old.

Summary

Have the partner who is leaving remove their belongings. It is very hard for children and partner either to have to live with discarded items or to live with visits made to collect them.

Both partners should be willing to discuss why the marriage broke up and to discuss with the children. Do not leave them guessing.

To maintain stability for the children it seems important for the outgoing partner to be sure to have a space in their new home for all the children.

Do not expect your children to cheer you on in a new partnership. They will be protective of the parent who is left and may genuinely not like the new person anyway.

Be sensitive to their feelings of displacement, 'not mattering', and jealousy of any new babies.

***

It will take longer than you ever imagined for the family to settle down again.

Personal experience

My children are grown up adults and had all left home when we split up. For this reason, they were not aware of how intolerable the situation had become. We were always at our best when the children were around, focusing on them rather than our differences.

Friends, however, were aware of something going on, and we were horrified to discover that several of them had been questioning the children about our situation. Worse, one of them actually asked our older daughter if we were splitting up. With no prior inkling, this was very upsetting for her and she bravely asked us what was happening. At that time we had not openly discussed separating so there was nothing to tell her. But the truth is that people pick up discord long before it *has* been discussed and the community suspects before the children may notice.

What we had forgotten is that adult children are part of the parent's community. We needed to inform them much earlier on because they had unwittingly become the communication source between the rest of the world and the family. None of them were giving the same answers, and they really are the first who need to be informed.

There can be no 'good' way of telling your children that their parents are not going to live together any more. You can do your best to soften the blow. Try walking in their shoes (or perhaps you went through it yourself as a child); be considerate, informative and loving. Tell them all together so that no one is left out of the loop. They are bound to talk about it together, so if they have all heard the same thing at the same time they can keep each other right if one of them has misheard.

When they asked how I was, at first I made the mistake of sharing with them as adults, and because I am honest I gave them the good and the bad. They didn't want to know. They stopped asking and we got in the crazy position of cheery conversations when really I was a mess.

What they did ask for was 'sign posts'. They did not want a blow by blow account of events but they did want to know where we had got to. I would type out a 'round robin' giving our position on house, finances, state of mind and job hunting, etc. It was only sent after my husband and I were in agreement about what we had written.

Each child responded differently, according to where they were in the five stages of loss. One always said thank you. The other two were often silent, which had me inquire if they had received it and if there was anything they wanted to say or ask. It was also clear there would be no offers of help to house-hunt, pack up, move and decision-make.

***

Do not expect your children to help you house-hunt, pack up, move and decision-make.

Friends

What a gift friends are, and how I have relied on them! Many of our friends have been party to our marital disputes and upsets. Some thought it would never come to this and some had been expecting it for years. We thought it prudent to let them know that we were separating. We did this at the beginning when we had different addresses, and we also made the circumstances clear. We did not want rumours, misinformation and the grape-vine working.

***

> **If you do not want rumours keep friends and family informed of circumstances.**

The feedback from this was that friends knew where we stood and where they stood. They knew that they were not required in any way to take sides, that they could communicate with both of us and still see each of us. As a result most of our friends remain 'ours', not his or mine. By letting them know we were still talking there was no burden on them about whom to invite to what. We would get our individual invitations with our host knowing if we both accepted that we would not wreck their event!

You will need some support, some shoulders to cry on and some ears to bend. Spread it around! For example, ask the financier about money, discuss the relevant topic with those who can help you best, do not expect your best friend to have all the answers you need, and remember that everybody brings their own expectations, beliefs, opinions and judgements to the situation. You will be too frazzled to sift through most of their suggestions, so let it go over your head and keep your eye clearly on your own goals. How you do it may not be how they would do it, and this does not make your way wrong.

Family

I do think it difficult for your families to remain impartial. Do not expect it of them and do not court their support either – it only makes it harder. Nevertheless they will undoubtedly be there for you; you can count on them, and they know you well.

I was particularly keen that the in-laws also knew that we were still in communication. I had known them all for thirty-five years and felt very incomplete when their contact stopped, and it was easy for me to believe that they had taken sides and were blocking me out. I then realized that perhaps they did not know what to do in this situation, so I sent round an update with my new address. I had a deluge of letters including an invitation to a wedding. I was thrilled to get this opportunity to go to a function and show that we were still talking, that we could be civilized and caring of each other and I had not set out to ruin their brother's life. I was included in the family photo, which moved me to tears.

7. Money

Money, that emotive topic!

How do you handle money? Are you generous or do you hoard? Do you speculate, or do you avoid anything to do with it and leave bills unopened? Which way does your partner do it? Indeed, what do you accuse them of over money? The clash over money seems to arise when we handle it differently from our partners. Each believes they are right, and this results in fears, control, bullying, threats and even bribes.

***

Get informed about your money and the state of it.

This is the time to get informed. If you are in a relationship where your partner handles your financial affairs you will need to find out everything. Get informed about your own money and the state of it, and get informed about your partner's money and the state of it.

What you can do

As your number one step start keeping a record of what you spend each month. You will be asked. If you go to a Mediator you will be given a form to fill and hand in. If you go to a lawyer, he will ask you, so you need to know. On this will be based all the calculations of what you will need to live.

Keep a little book with you and jot down every paper you buy, taxis, coffees, beers, etc. Here are some categories to jog your mind:

· **Transport**: bus, taxi, flights, parking, trains, tubes

· **Car**: petrol, parking permit, insurance, servicing, mot, licence, road tax

· **Food**: housekeeping, meals out

· **Entertainment**: cinema, theatre, books, hobbies

· **Leisure**: sport, golf, fishing etc. evening classes, pub, newspapers/mag

· **Body**: gym, hair, beauty clinic, cigarettes

· **Clothing**: formal and informal, shoes and accessories

· **Shopping**: Chemist, Post Office, birthdays, holidays, gifts.

Other categories include your monthly outgoings:

· **Direct debits and standing orders**: Gas, Electricity, Rates, Mortgage, Insurance, pension, savings, tax, charities, etc.

· **Occasional outgoings:** dentist, doctor, glasses, prescriptions

· **Children**: uniform, clothes, extra lessons, dinner money, school outings, etc.

You will also need to list:

· ISAs

· Stocks and shares

· Speculative investments

· Deposit and other savings accounts

· Joint accounts

· Properties, Holiday Homes, Timeshares

· Anything else you own

All of these will need valuations as of the date you separated. Phone your ISA account managers, explain why you want a valuation and it will be sent to you. You will need to hand this in. For deposit accounts you can also give a date, and a valuation will be calculated and posted to you. You can save valuable time if you arrive at meetings with this information to hand.

***

> **Save valuable time and expense by arriving at
> meetings with facts and information to hand.**

Joint holdings

Divide your joint account now. Also, make sure that any spare or other joint deposited savings cannot be moved, hidden or spent on defunct causes without your knowledge.

Pensions

You will need to find out the specific rules of your pension company. You need to know their policy about the age that the pension can be redeemed, how large the cash lump sum, and the annuity pay out amount. These rules will enable you to figure out how to achieve a clean break if you want one, or whether it makes sense to share the pension and take an annual payout. A clean break means you want a settlement now, without later payouts.

The law in Britain is being amended to catch up with Scotland where the value of the pension is taken into account; it is taken as part of the matrimonial property and therefore to be split between you. You can agree to take your share of the pension at a later date, providing you can exist on what else you will get. Many people balk at taking their pension now because it may mean cashing it in long before they are ready. The longer it is left intact, the more it will grow.

The valuing of pensions is a complicated business. Tax may be taken into consideration but you are likely to receive 40-45% of the pension, not an amount that your spouse and their lawyer think they can get away with. If you are uncomfortable with any of the calculations done you can get an independent actuary report, which is what will be used in legislation if you go to court. At the moment the law says that only in divorce can your spouse 'earmark' part of a lump sum on his retirement. He can also refuse to take a lump sum.

***

> **Valuing of pensions can be complicated. Get an independent report.**

Do not be afraid of going to court. It will be fair. You will, however, need to consider divorce lawyers' fees versus court fees.

Government Pension

If you are not sure what you have contributed over the years, or if you do not know how much you will get on your retirement, visit www.nidirect.gov.uk. You will need your National Insurance number if you have it. You can work out an outline of your situation and any recommendations about you topping it up with a lump sum if you are behind on payments.

If you have never contributed you are entitled to a percentage of your husband's pension, which will be calculated right up to the moment you have a decree absolute, and for which they need the date of the decree and your husband's National Insurance number. It is one of those government niceties that in order to get your share of the basic state pension you are entitled to you *have* to divorce.

Consider Maintenance vs Lump Sum

Look at the implications of instalments of payments from capital. It is likely to be taxed, whereas a periodical allowance is regarded as maintenance and would therefore be tax-free.

Learn your tax position, now and when you will be on your own. Count it into your reckoning.

If you decide to sell the family home and the transaction is completed before you have an agreement, the money can be frozen. By what amount does this reduce what you will have to live off if this situation arises?

Do a reality test

When you have gathered all your information, do a 'reality test'. Having kept your spending record you now know what you need in order to live per month. Have some fun dividing the money every which way and seeing what you can come up with.

Create pages of different scenario splits: Can you keep your house? Is there enough in the pot to pay you out without touching the pension? Can you get a job and a wage? If not, how can you create an income? etc. etc. (see chapter on 'Decision-Making Procedures').

Personal experience

Once more I picked the brains of friends who had been through this. What solution had they settled on and was it working for them? Just how much did they need? There were many horror stories of their periodical allowances drying up once a new partner came on the scene.

I began by wanting the security of our pension scheme paying me something per year for the rest of my life. This felt safe and cosy, but then I noticed how restrictive it was as well. All that money tied up for a payout that might not keep up with the cost of living. I would rather have it in cash now and see if I could double it!

Nor did I fancy being controlled over money for an indeterminate time, i.e. when I may have it, and how much. I had visions of being put off for maybe ten years because I seemed to be doing okay, and therefore didn't it make sense to leave the pension untouched for as long as possible? As I was wanting my freedom, I wanted it complete. I have things I want to do in my life now – not go on waiting and waiting till I am decrepit. We got round this by my husband being willing to borrow in order to pay me out my share of his pension.

The best question I was asked was, "Do you want to live your life frugally, eking out your share and wondering if it will see you out - or do you want to live your life to the full and use what you get to create more?" Each time I got scared I reminded myself I want to live my life to the full, right here, right now.

Checklist

- Keep a record of what you spend
- Divide your joint accounts
- Check out your private pensions
- Get your government pension forecast done
- Consider maintenance vs lump sum
- Do a reality test

8. Communicating

Using a tool to enable you to reach an agreement, without either of you giving in, is what creates a win/win outcome.

It is extremely easy in disputes to make the other person wrong because they are not thinking our way, because they do not agree with us, and, maybe, because their method of sorting it out doesn't make sense to us. How do you behave when this happens? It is too easy to sit in blame, and not acknowledge that we all have some irritating traits. We are *all* a little bit difficult and have some habits we annoy others with – and sometimes even ourselves!

Taking Positions

This is the most common form of arguing. One side takes up a position and then gets locked into it. The other side takes a different position and the sparring begins.

The more you defend your position the harder it is to give it up. We then find ourselves trapped in a corner of our own making with no obvious way out without – we believe – giving in, giving up or 'losing face'.

***

> There is no question that agreement will become less and less likely if more attention is paid to the position than to the problem that began the dispute in the first place.

Separating the Problem from the Person

In family matters the relationship becomes tangled up with the dispute. Quarrels over a relatively inconsequential point may escalate into an emotional dogfight. Thus statements about the 'untidiness of the sitting room', and 'no-one helping with taking the rubbish out', may be factual but are likely to be taken as a personal attack.

Such comments may get defended – and attack follows, counter-defence, more attack, and soon it *does* become personal. The point at issue is lost, the problem requiring sorting out has sunk beneath mud-slinging and before you know what has happened the relationship is under fire, *not* the problem!

Opinions versus Facts

You will have experienced different opinions frequently. The trick is to separate out identifiable, verifiable data from this opinion. There is no doubt that some people are superb at presenting an opinion *as* fact. Unless you have the facts yourself, you will have very little ground to negotiate from which will leave you believing you are powerless and that you 'gave in'.

***

> **Unless you have the facts and data for yourself, you will have very little ground from which to negotiate.**

Thus, when you are negotiating the terms of your separation agreement, from furniture to alimony, and you do not understand or have the full facts about anything, say so, and then get them. Your partner's statement/opinion could be made from a thin knowledge base, poor memory, a guess, or second-hand information. Wherever the opinion has come from, it makes enough sense to your partner that it is repeated to you in a tone and manner which sends the message to you that 'this is a fact'.

Many years ago, my widowed mother had exchanged with us her large cutlery canteen for our smaller one. When we separated my husband thought that this item was now ours and therefore jointly owned and that he would like it. This opinion was presented to me as a fact, and I felt very wobbly since it had been a wedding present to my mother and I would have liked to keep it in my side of the family.

I checked out Mother's memory about it. In fact, her cutlery canteen was only on long loan to us. We could exchange back again at any time. Since our set of cutlery has an inscribed 'S' on it she had never planned to keep it anyway and was only helping us out at the time. When we got our own set back again, this was the jointly owned one for division – *not*

Mother's set. We resolved it by my husband taking our wedding set with the 'S' on. I did keep Mother's set and I bought her a replacement.

This outcome is what I consider a win/win. We all got what we wanted but it took separating out fact from opinion before we could negotiate and create this conclusion.

Listening

One of the skills of communication is listening. Most of us think we are pretty good listeners. To listen well is hard work – it is a question of attitude and concentration. If we can't be bothered to make the effort, listening simply becomes what we do while waiting our turn to speak.

***

> **If we do not make the effort to listen with concentration, listening simply becomes what we do while waiting our turn to speak.**

You have probably experienced not being listened to. This is obvious when the other looks away, fidgets, avoids eye contact and doesn't respond verbally in any way – or worse, responds inappropriately.

Less obvious is the person who is mentally thinking out their counter-argument in their head. You can't see this happening but it becomes clear you have not been listened to when they speak. Some may interrupt you because they want to have their say so badly; this does not allow you to express your complete thoughts and you may feel annoyed, hurt and certainly not heard.

So, if you have been on the receiving end of these types of communication you will know how frustrating it is. However, the issue is, are you any better? How do you measure up as a listener? Ask yourself the following questions:

· Do I look at my partner when they are speaking?

· Do I allow my partner to express his or her complete thoughts without interrupting?

· Do I separate fact from opinion?

· Do I identify key points and remember them?

· Do I listen between the lines, especially if my partner often uses hidden meanings?

· Do I avoid becoming hostile or excited when my partner's views differ from my own?

· Do I opt out when the subject is something I do not really understand?

· Do I ignore distractions when listening?

· Do I repeat essential details back to my partner to ensure correct understanding?

There are a lot of books available to read about negotiation. In 1981 Roger Fisher and William Ury published a book called *Getting to Yes*. In this book they write about the different steps to take to 'negotiate an agreement without giving in'. These steps were then developed by Stephen Covey, The version presented here is what Dr K Bradford Brown of the More to Life Programme developed from couples work done by Dr John Hoover (Dr John Hoover and Dr K Brown have joint copyright).

I re-present here an exploration process that I have come to know as Baseball. In Britain the game of getting round bases is known as Rounders. Getting round these exploration bases requires you to use your skills as a listener, your ability to separate out facts, your common sense and above all the key ingredient of 'mirroring'.

What is 'mirroring'? This is your ability to retain key facts and tell them back to your partner. In other words you feed back to your partner, in your own words, *exactly* what they have said, with no interruptions, no "Yes but…" and above all no interpretations, judgements or evaluations. The importance here, is for the other to *know* they have been heard by you, all the way down.

This is enormously defusing and settling. The dispute will take on a different perspective and you will find you can move towards an agreement together.

***

Your ability to retain key facts and tell them back to your partner is enormously defusing and settling.

A model of NON-COMMUNICATION

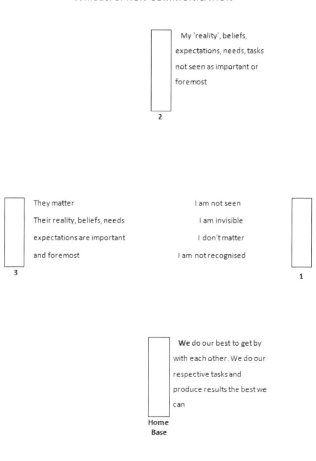

Let's look at the steps (bases) 1, 2, 3 and Home Base in the game of Baseball/Rounders pattern when we do *not* communicate at each base.

And this is how the bases can be when we are communicating well:

A model of COMMUNICATION

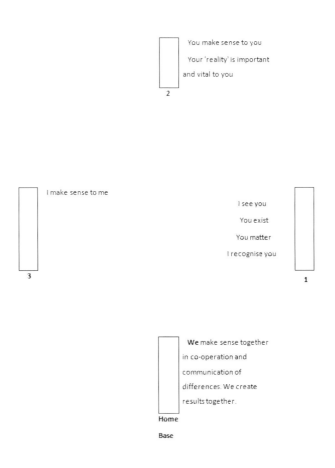

You make sense to you
Your 'reality' is important
and vital to you

2

I make sense to me

I see you
You exist
You matter
I recognise you

3

1

We make sense together
in co-operation and
communication of
differences. We create
results together.

Home

Base

Now you are ready to learn the steps of Baseball/Rounders so that you can create the outcomes you want in your life. You can create them without conflict, without winning, without either side 'losing face'. You will retain your dignity, grace and free will. You will hear your partner's sense of the incident/event/dispute. You know you make sense, so now your decisions can be based on common sense.

You will need to prepare.

Remind yourself that inside of your partner is a human being of nobility and worth. That once you shared a lot and that he/she mattered to you. This can be hard if you are now resentful and hurting but I assure you this is a vital step in the process. (It may help you to do the Cost Process first as outlined in chapter on 'Resentment versus Regrets'.) This step will get you back in touch with that good and noble part of yourself, your Higher Self, who as Wayne Dyer suggests, would 'Wish to work this out from your purest intentions and the greater good of all.'

These are the steps round the bases in how to COMMUNICATE and create a WIN/ WIN outcome:

EXPLORATION PROCESS

1. *Honouring:*

Get to first base by establishing that you have unconditional positive regard for your partner. In order for the other to feel visible and that they matter, you might list the attributes you honour and respect in them.

You do this by remembering the person right now (not the problem).

2. *THEY make sense:*

Hear their concerns. They make sense to themselves even though they may not make sense to you. It is important that you communicate that *they* make sense. Try phrases such as "Tell me what happened..." or "Tell me more about it..."

b) Mirror/reflect their reality. Remember this is how it was for *them*: no confrontation, interruptions or "Yes but..." no evaluations or judgements.

Suggested phrases you could use:

"You want me to know that..."

"I understand that for *you* it is that..."

When your partner senses they are fully heard, ask, "Is there anything else you want me to understand?"

3. *YOU make sense:*

Verify what has been said, if appropriate. Share what you know. How it was for you: *you* also make sense.

REMEMBER - As you use this tool in life, if communication does *not* open up go back to Base 2. Keep hearing your partner and keep mirroring back what they have said. When the other person believes they are heard then they will be ready to hear *you* at Base 3.

Home Base

We *both* make sense.

Use phrases such as:

"Here's my suggestion…"

"What do we want to do?"

"How might we work this out?…"

"What compromises do we want?"

"Let's…"

BASEBALL/ROUNDERS

THE MODEL OF HOW TO COMMUNICATE AND CREATE A WIN/ WIN OUTCOME

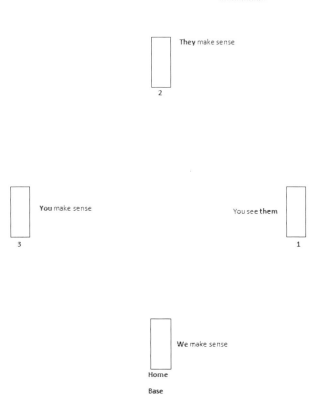

They make sense

2

You make sense

3

You see them

1

We make sense

Home
Base

In every area of your life there will be disputes, misunderstandings, parental conflict and differences of opinion all needing to be sorted out. Your relationships with colleagues, partner, relatives and children will wax and wane from friendly to hostile. How these entanglements can be amicably resolved is often the willingness of one party to take the trouble to use their listening and negotiating skills.

***

> **Entanglements can be amicably resolved by the willingness of one party to take the trouble to use their listening and negotiating skills.**

The communication tool just described is an extremely effective method of defusing conflict. There is no doubt that once emotions are settled down by being understood for what they are – just emotions – you can then focus on the problem with some clarity. This is not about denying emotions, because they are real and painful. But emotions fog our thinking and then our logic disappears. Therefore they are not a sound basis from which to make a decision.

***

> **Emotions can fog our thinking and then our logic disappears. Therefore they are not a sound basis from which to make a decision.**

And some of the decisions you will be making at this time will be of the utmost importance - decisions about your children's wellbeing, their future, your future, your home, your money, etc. You will find that playing Baseball/Rounders will help you to create outcomes for all of you that you can live with. It is an extraordinarily effective tool.

The good news is you can play it and the other person need not even be aware of the bases that you are leading them round. I urge you to try it.

9. Property and Belongings

So what do you own?

Your property may be valued as a large part of your estate. Your home is probably the single biggest investment you have made. You will be asked its value, mortgage, resale etc.

Are you renting or do you own your home? Is there a mortgage? Inform yourself on your exact mortgage payments, the length of time to run, how much and to whom. Is the mortgage transferable if you stay in the home, even if at the moment you are not the mortgage payer? Will you have to take out a new mortgage and with what?

***

> **You will need to have the house valued by a surveyor. A guess at market prices will not do.**

You will need to have the house valued by a surveyor. A guess at market prices will not do. There may be a discrepancy between the survey value and what you would actually get on the market. In your calculations you may have to agree to adjust the amount up or down whether you sell or keep it.

Note

If you are selling your joint house and purchasing another place for yourself be aware of the house-sale money becoming frozen. If you do not have your separation agreements in place, to whom should the house agent pay over the money? As I was due the house sale money in our settlement, I put in an offer on a flat for myself. This was accepted but if I hadn't got the house money how was I going to pay for it? We got round this by both our individual lawyers writing to the house agent saying that I was due the house money, and only then did he hand over the cheque. In the event we did not sign the agreement for a further two months but at least I was not in the position of paying for an expensive bridging loan in the interim.

Do you have Timeshare, a holiday home, a commuter's *pied-a-terre*, a caravan or a boat? Do you have a field and a horse? What is the value of your car? All these will require valuations. Even if you have agreed who will have what, you will need a respected valuation so there are no comebacks later.

Once you have the agreed price on items, you will get a clearer picture of your total worth and therefore how to split it fairly. For instance, we had one car and now we would require two. Do you sell the one and buy two, or does one of you keep it and the other purchase? You are each entitled to half of the car's current value. My husband wanted to keep the car so I chose a second-hand car. He put towards it the half

I was owed on our current car and I paid the balance. In this way I now have a car of better value than I could otherwise have afforded.

Belongings, including furniture

(See also the chapter on 'Decision-Making Procedures' on how to make your list, and tips)

Your Mediator or lawyer will want a present-day valuation on your house contents. This is expensive and unnecessary in my view, as one or both of you has been purchasing for your home for a number of years and will be familiar with current costs, bargains and replacement costs. It seemed to me that whichever spouse did not get the dining room table was going to have to buy one. What was the point in valuing the old one at £250 when it would cost upwards of £600 to replace it?

I suggest you try the following:

· Go through your possessions and split out what your partner brought to the marriage and what you brought. These may be items from your bachelor pad or given you from your childhood home as gifts along the way. Technically they are jointly owned. However, are you really going to fight for that lovely desk and old oak chest which came from his home? It's just the same as you feeling possessive about the brass bedstead and sideboard you grew up with and do not want to part with. Ask your higher self: Can you not let him have his stuff with love?

· If you can do this, even if it is not absolutely

equal, list these things on one side and do not include them in the valuation.

· You are now left with your joint items. List them and put your idea of price beside them. This may seem an onerous task but it has to be done, and you can save a huge amount of money doing it yourself. This is the point where you give today's valuation: what will it cost you to buy another one? Your ancient beloved faithful old Hoover washing machine is worth £20 scrap, but you are looking at £200–£300 to buy another, less good make.

By doing it this way you are going to know exactly what it is going to cost you to set up home. Now you start the division. This is painful emotionally. Stay practical as there will be pieces you are longing for and pieces you know you do not want.

At your first shot at this stand back and do it detachedly. Do not get side-tracked into emotional outbursts of affection for the coal scuttle. Such comments as, "You don't even have a fireplace," hold no weight. Attachment to an object is entirely without reason.

***

> **Be willing to acknowledge that your partner bought certain items because they loved them and would like to have them.**

Take into consideration items one of you has

bought because they loved it and therefore would like to get it, such as pictures or holiday purchases. In this way you will finish up with very little to dispute over.

Disputes

There are several solutions to disputes. Remember that you are looking for solutions that will enable you to accept them without resentment and beliefs of unfairness.

Here are a few:

· Adding up the valuations on one side may result in being seriously down on the other. It could be balanced by an expensive piece of furniture being given up to the other side.

· You can trade with each other.

· You could draw straws if you are gamblers.

· You could take it in turns to choose.

· You could buy a piece from the other.

· You could sell it and neither of you have it.

· You could give it to your children.

· You could take it in turns to have it.

· You could give it up on condition that if the other finds no use for it at any time you will be offered it.

· You could put it on one side to be given to a child as a wedding present.

· You could divide it. For example a large dinner

service could give you both something to eat off until one of you has purchased another. Then either of you could hand over the other half so the set is complete again.

None of these solutions is bizarre if it enables you to do it without rancour.

10. Decision-Making Procedures

This chapter shares with you some of the actual processes we used and how to set out the piece of paper.

Uppermost for you may be the burning question, "Do I have to move or can I stay in my home?" I get very attached to my houses and extremely sentimental about leaving them. This is the seat of decision-making problems. Once our emotions are involved, our 'thinker' - our logic - is literally out of action. I went round and round exploring taking in lodgers, doing bed and breakfast, and dividing the property... how could I make it viable to stay because I was sentimentally attached?

***

> **Once our emotions are involved, our 'thinker', our logic, is literally out of action.**

On waking one night and churning once more I sat up and listed all the options. In the morning, I took a sheet of paper and divided it into four portions. I labelled each quadrant with a heading:

'PROS', 'CONS', 'Logic' and 'Emotion'. Taking a clean sheet for each option I filled in the four quadrants. It was amazing how quickly it became clear what to do. It became obvious where I was being overemotional, and my logic could return so that I could clearly see where and how I could make money, live, etc. I did not try and stay in the house, which would have tied up all my settlement capital and forced me to make the house earn for me. Another option revealed that for me to buy a smaller place, take in a lodger and invest remaining capital was far more acceptable. When I could clearly see this logic, making the decision to leave my home was then easier.

***

Make decisions from a clear, logical space.

House contents

Now you have decisions to make about the house contents.

Dividing a home is a daunting task. In our case every single item had five potential answers. Was it his, was it mine, was it one of three children's, was it OK for a charity shop, or was it rubbish. The thought of it all overwhelmed me. Where to begin?

Go from room to room, making an inventory. Open all the cupboards. Go to the attic, the garage and the garden shed. This ranges from tedious to upsetting. When I did it, I wondered whether to list items in groups, e.g. all linen, all glassware, all china. I decided my visual memory preferred to leave things where they were so that when my husband asked about a long-forgotten item I could go straight to it (and also show I had not rushed out and sold it!). If you have a computer now is the time to draw up your furniture list on an Excel spreadsheet. This will save a lot of rewriting when you start moving things to different columns and pricing items. If you cannot use a spreadsheet, list your furniture by room first.

As discussed in the property chapter, I suggest you separate out what you consider yours (or theirs) because you (or they) brought it to the marriage. Now you are left with jointly owned items. If you can, go round the rooms together saying what you want. How to do this is also in the Property chapter.

· On your spreadsheet head up your columns and move the items to the correct one.

· Now price each item.

· Now add it up.

You will quickly see if there is a bias one way. Set about trading with each other or one of the suggestions also listed in Property chapter. Make further columns headed 'Gifts', 'To sell', and 'Designate to children'. If neither of you want it you can sell it either in an auction house or a garage or car-boot sale. I suggest you do your pricing as outlined in Property chapter. When you have a semblance of agreement you will have a figure to put on your property sheet for the Mediator or lawyers.

You are doing well. You have a decision and price on your house. You now also have some decisions and prices on your belongings. As other assets are added to your total list of ownership, I suggest you create another spreadsheet and list all your finances and assets; this might include separate categories for your mortgage, loans, credit cards etc. Add them up.

Reality test

Now do a 'reality test'. This is for you to look at what money and possessions you will have and work out if you can exist. Will you have somewhere to live? Can you furnish it? Will you have an income? Remember taxes. Does it look good on paper but in reality is unviable? I found that some speculative ventures were being put in my column that I did not want. They were not earning, were unsellable, and certainly would not feed me. I could not base my existence on a venture that might never come good. In the end we agreed he would keep the ventures, and if they came good, lucky him. Instead I would be given the equivalent price in cash. Now I can eat whether I am employed or not, and he has got a good job and some speculative investments. These things are solvable.

I doubt you will be able to do any of this part of your separation in a hurry. It took us twelve hours just to divide the accumulation of photograph albums. I have known partners walk away from this part saying, "Take it all," and have then left. Done with pride and anger at the time, they are full of regret and resentment now. The aim is to come out of this still talking, and money and belongings are the most charged areas of the entire process.

***

> **The aim is to come out of this still talking, and
> money and belongings are the most charged areas of
> the entire process.**

If you have been left and everything went with them, you are entitled to fight for what is yours. You are due half the estate, so even if you never see your belongings again you will be paid for them. The courts will be fair.

DECISION-MAKING

Decision to be made...

PROs	CONs
EMOTIONAL	LOGIC

11. Dis-ease versus Disease

I would like to give you some information about how dis-ease becomes disease. Frequently it begins with anger and depression. Some depressions are *suppressed* anger. If you think of anger as the fulcrum of a seesaw you will note that it can go both ways – up or down. Thus, suppressed anger spirals down into mild depression, mood swings, black holes, and deep depression – even, in the extreme, to suicide. Alternatively, your temperament may be the other side of the fulcrum and you *express* your anger. This comes out as annoyance, irritation, anger and rage, overwrought behaviour and out-of-control fury – even, in the extreme, as murder.

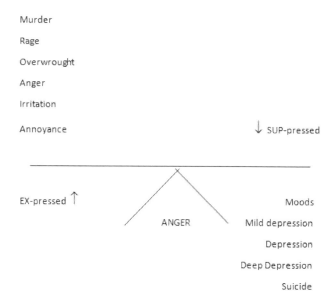

Murder
Rage
Overwrought
Anger
Irritation
Annoyance   ↓ SUP-pressed

EX-pressed ↑   Moods
                         ANGER   Mild depression
                                                 Depression
                                             Deep Depression
                                                   Suicide

Getting help

Do get help. You do not have to struggle alone with uncontrollable emotions. You need to be able to function and there are many drugs to help you temporarily over this difficult time. I am not the depressed type; I bounce. However, I can and do express anger, and I got so totally overwrought that I hardly knew which way up I was. Unfortunately my GP kept suggesting herbal remedies, which were far too mild to help me in my state. After an hysterical display in the surgery it was agreed I could try happy pills. (St. John's Wort is a good herbal alternative which may help some of you.) Oh, the relief not to be in tears all the time and to regain some kind of sleep pattern. I could function rationally. I wish I had been given this sooner, as some very unpleasant experiences might have been avoided.

Do not think of pill-taking as some kind of failure. I do not have my self-esteem attached to 'bracing up' and coping. If there is something invented to temporarily help me, thank you, I will use it, monitor myself and then move on. Try it for yourself.

12. Looking After You

How are your mind, your body and your soul doing?

Is your mind churning, working overtime and worrying at things like a dog with a bone?

Is your body exhausted, listless, getting sick or hyper-energetic?

Is your soul at ease? Or are you praying like never before, or have you given up on G.O.D.?

There is now no doubt that the state of your mind affects the state of your body. However, despite the fact that we know this, rising above both to find your higher self isn't necessarily getting any easier.

The mind

Your mind is that commentary running in your head at all times. It rattles away with opinions, beliefs, judgements, interpretations, expectations, hopes and fears. With each daily event your mind will be busy and you will be reacting. The trouble is we act out of these interpretations many times without checking if we are correct. Thus misunderstandings, crossed wires, and arguments abound, when often what is required is verification of a situation or a phrase. It is also true that our interpretations are based on past experiences that colour our reaction now. Can you notice you doing this?

Your body

Your body will tell you what is going on. Your reaction to an event, a situation, a phrase or even a look is the result of your mind's interpretation. The adrenaline rush, butterflies in the tummy, sweaty palms and little breath is your body reacting to what your mind is telling it. The point is, is what you are telling yourself true? Whatever you are telling yourself can be checked out. Just ask.

Your soul

I call my soul my higher self, that part of me which is wise, that part of me which is very old and knows. When we are caught in painful situations and emotions it is easy to react from a place of hate, disrespect and disdain. Is this who you really are? Is this what your higher self would say or do?

Dis-ease

Let us return to your mind. How big a hold has it got on you? Are you distracted most of the time with imaginary conversations in your head? Do you wake at 3.00 a.m., churning? Are you so short of sleep you are snapping at anyone within range?

Dis-ease, which we can name as insomnia,

constipation, migraine, ulcers, stomach cramps, flatulence *et al,* can be laid at the door of the mind. So how can we respond to the mind instead of reacting so violently?

Truth-telling

Firstly, I recommend teaching yourself the principal of verification. The mind likes to makes generalisations and may insert the word 'always'. For instance, if you forgot your house keys last Tuesday, your mind, that voice in your head, will accuse you of *always* being forgetful when in fact, you were only forgetful last Tuesday. It is false that you are 'always' forgetful.

In a separation situation your mind may be busy telling you that you are a failure, stupid, unlovable. Your mind may also be making up things about your partner, that he/she is cruel, mean, selfish. Ask yourself the 'always' question. Is it true or false, or is it a 'don't know' that I am 'always' stupid? How about your partner? Is he/she really 'always' mean? Was that furtive phone call, which made you suspicious, actually made to their lover? Do you honestly *know* how they will react or behave in any situation? So often we think we know, we are sure we know, but when truthful with ourselves, we can admit we don't know. You can save yourself considerable heartache by checking out the facts, instead of jumping to the wrong conclusion. When you have correct data, *then* you can respond and react appropriately.

Talking

In all times of dis-ease it helps to talk. Have you thought of having counselling? There are many different formats and styles of counselling; find one that suits you. What you are looking for is a good impartial listener. Do not expect your best friend to play this role, because they cannot help but bring their own baggage to the situation. Nor can they fix it.

Writing

Perhaps you prefer to write. Read *The Artist's Way* by Julia Cameron, who provides a chapter-by-chapter route to make you whole again. The first rule is to write what she calls 'morning pages' – a minimum of three pages to be written on waking. Keep the pen moving, do not censor yourself, and just pour down on paper all you need to. There is no right or wrong way and no one else will read it. It is both cathartic and clarifying.

Personal development

You could take a self-development course. Go and learn about yourself and the games you play. Learn to recognize others' games and how to handle them. How is your self-esteem right now? Pretty low would be my guess (see courses at the back of this book).

There are many tapes you can listen to. Some handle anger, resentments etc. Use anything available to you to help you keep your mind clear.

Physical fitness

Are you ignoring your body? After those adrenaline rushes do you exercise the adrenaline away or has it pocketed in your muscles, leaving you listless? If you belong to a gym, use it. Whatever you normally do, keep it up.

Ask friends what helped them. I discovered massages, herbal tea, calming herbal pills and a host of other remedies. Try all of it and then settle into a routine which your body will appreciate and respond to. My insomnia improved rapidly by doing something new to me. I now take a long evening soak in the bath – lavender drops in the water, soothing music on the tape, a cup of night time herbal tea, and I am ready for sleep!

Nurturing the Soul

And finally, find recreation for your soul. Again, do what fits for you, what feeds and nurtures your inner being. Return to church or drop it. Pray again or discover meditation. If smells, bells and whistles suit you, have them. If you want to embrace a new philosophy, religion or worship, guardian angels and/or, Indian Medicine cards then do so. Ignore comments that you have lost the plot! Your soul knows what it needs and will tell you if you listen. Again, try some of the many excellent tapes available.

I was given a *Manifesting* tape by Wayne Dyer which I played after I had written my morning pages. I loved his soothing voice encouraging me to visualize what I wanted in my life and the changes I wanted to make. I got out of bed each day with renewed hope.

You can too.

Your Higher Self

Do your best to stay in touch with this part of you –
this strong, noble and wise self. Let it be your guide.
What you want from this separation is the best for all of
you. Caught in your pain and misery, your psychological
self may be burning for revenge but your higher self
would prefer harmony. If you are the leaver you may be
feeling profound relief to be out of the relationship,
please remember the other's pain and ask yourself 'how
can I respond to this situation with love?'

This is hard, so try this:

· Take a breath; then take another one and say to
yourself, "This too will pass."

· When you have calmed down go *towards* your fear.

I can promise you, from my own experience, that
every time I managed to move towards what I
dreaded, every time I stepped into love, what I feared
most simply did not happen.

 Personal experience

My husband was spending time with my daughter
and grandchildren on holiday. I was able to let a pang
of jealousy go, because they were coming to stay with

me later. However, my husband and I still lived in the same city, and I had fears he would encroach on my time with them because he had indicated he wanted to see them again etc., etc. I churned on my possessiveness and hated myself for these selfish longings to have them all to myself. My higher self reminded me that:

· The children loved me with or without Dad

· This was likely to be a one off

· We had reared them together

· It might even be nice for them to have us together again. I could manage it with love and harmony.

Well, what do you think happened? My husband brought forward his hernia operation, took himself off into hospital and then went away to convalesce. The situation of my fear did not arise. If I had tried to control the situation, if I had come at it with resentment and annoyance, I guarantee the universe would have given me what I did not want, because that's how life teaches us to do things differently.

I have more and more incidents of not getting what I dread if I can go towards it with love. Try it for yourself. Good luck.

13. Regrets versus Resentments

'In relationships, 'resentment' is the real four-letter word.'

- K Bradford Brown

What is regret? It is the feeling which goes with something unfinished, something we have said or done which we wish we hadn't. The feeling is of sadness, remorse or even shame. It is the genuine deep feeling of being sorry and it is often accompanied by tears.

***

> **Regret is the genuine deep feeling of being sorry. Resentments are feelings of ill will, often held over a very long time.**

What is resentment? Resentments are feelings of ill will, often held over a very long time and with good reason. They are made from the injustices we have stored up through our lives and hung onto so that we can blame someone else for our condition. Something awful may have happened to you or been said to you or about you. The problem is we then add more on.

We see slights, innuendos, inferences and more hurts round every corner. Then, we can sit full of justification, playing out martyrdom, 'poor me', victim, and a host of other 'dramas' which enable us to make the other person wrong. It is that Gladstone bag of dead cats that we lug around with us, pulling one out if someone will listen. They smell. Moreover, the other person often won't remember the slight, the incident or the circumstance, yet you may have been harbouring ill will towards them for many years. This ill will is called the 'cost'. What has it cost you?

The only reason that we hang onto resentment is because we get something from doing so. Something that strokes us and makes us feel right and the other person wrong. This stroke is called your 'payoff'. What are you getting?

Over fifteen years of many varied self-development courses I have taken, the best process I have found for shifting resentments is that developed by the More to Life programme. I have searched other courses and religions and I know of no other which will get you into a space of forgiveness that *stays*. All the others I have explored can deliver the potential to forgive, but when I scratch the surface up will come the old resentment; it has not gone, nor is it much dissipated.

By kind permission of Dr K Bradford Brown, co-founder of More to Life Programme, who holds the copyright for the following material, I have written out *The Cost Process* and how to do it. Normally this process is learned alongside other people learning the same thing, and there is a strong sense of companionship which helps enormously. Even so, I hope that simply by doing it as it is described here, it makes the difference to you that it has to me, because it is through doing this work we can discover our true power and re-assert our ability to love.

The Cost Process Steps

1. *Confess the full extent of your resentment*
2. *Share your payoff*
3. *Share your cost*
4. *Ask for and offer forgiveness*
5. *Commit to a new intention or action*

When to do this process

The Cost Process illuminates our resentments, some of which may have been held over a very long period of time. The time to do a Cost Process is whenever you become aware of resentment or ill will towards another person. The process shows us how to disengage ourselves from the attraction of making ourselves good, righteous, superior and powerful at other people's expense.

You may find it helpful to do this with a friend who would be willing to take you through these steps as presented. The person you are working on is in front of you in your *imagination*; this is *not* about dumping on them face to face.

Practicing the process

1. Confess the extent of the resentment

This process is done in relation to a specific person that is resented. This person may have done hurtful, shitty things to you.

Next, *picture* the person in question in front of you. *Now tell them the full extent of your resentment. Tell how you have held this person in your mind, what you have said or thought about them, how your resentment has shown itself. It will include things you have said to them and done to them i.e. 'put downs', exposure, getting others into agreement with you, being cruel, dismissive etc.*

(This is not a process in which you rant at the person or justify your own behaviour or blame the other person. It is easy to slip into this attitude if you aren't alert to this. Another major pitfall for many people occurs when they veer off and begin relating the cost of what the *other* person has done. For example, a woman doing the Cost Process on her father says, "I've never learned to relate to men because of how you treated me. It's your fault." This is blaming, not taking responsibility for your own part of the bitterness.)

2. Share the benefits

What have you *got* out of holding onto your resentment? We call this your 'payoff'.

To facilitate you in seeing the benefits/payoff you are getting from holding a resentment, ask yourself, "How do I get to feel when I believe they are…? What do I get to do? What do I get to avoid? What do I *not* have to do?"

Resentment is *never* held over time without a benefit/payoff. These benefits often include:

· **Being right**: You can be right and make the other person wrong and you can usually get support for your position. Agreement from friends reinforces your 'rightness'.

· **Self-righteousness**: Being morally superior to the other attracts attention, sympathy, and more agreement. "Poor me, look how I've been wronged… and I'm so good."

· **Doing it your way**: Resentment separates you and you may get to live your life alone, being apparently sufficient unto yourself.

· **Power/Control**: There is a false sense of 'power' that feeds resentment, and a fear of losing 'control' if resentment is given up. See how the fear of losing 'power/control' becomes a terrible cost to relationship, self-expression and spirituality.

· **Self-justification**: Resentments are often held because of a belief that the other person has damaged you in a way that you can never recover from. For example: "It's because of you I've never been able to have confidence in myself."

The big surprise of this process is that if the resentment is let go, the damage is healed. *It is the resentment itself which cripples*, not the event. If the resentment is given up then the healing is done. You see yourself as OK, and at last understand that you can't hide behind the other person's action any more. This is often a scary transition. "If I can't hide, I'll have to be responsible for my life!"

Watch for blame and keep working to see the bottom line belief that fuels the blame – the belief that the other person has damaged you in some permanent way. This belief needs to be seen for what it is: untrue.

3. Acknowledge the cost

Now, own the cost of your resentment, the price you have paid for holding the other person at fault, or wrong, and doing whatever you have done to them. Notice that another cost is that by holding onto this resentment you have kept the pain alive and not healed.

There are five major areas in which to look for cost:

· **Relationships**: How has this held resentment affected your ability to love and be loved? Your ability to trust, to care deeply, to be vulnerable?

· **Self-expression**: What has been the cost to your ability to express yourself? Resentments always hinder self-expression, and destroy our sense of well-being.

· **Health**: What has been the effect on your body in terms of tension, aches, pains, disease?

· **Sexuality**: What has been the cost to your

sexuality, your ability to function as a man or a woman in the world?

·   **Spirituality**: How has resentment affected your spiritual life, your relationship with your inner self, with your Creator, the universe, with the All (whatever your own word for that is)?

4. Forgiveness

Forgiveness is the absolute refusal to hold ill will towards another. Forgiving does not mean that you condone what they did or that what they said is okay.

Forgiveness just means that you are letting go of your resentment.

So, when the beliefs and cost have been explored and acknowledged, in your imagination, *offer forgiveness to the other person, and ask them to forgive you for holding the resentment against them for so long*. This step is usually easy, once the cost is fully realized and you can see how illusory the benefits really are.

If you simply cannot let go of the resentment, then exaggerate it, get into it more and more, keep telling the other person how you hate them and what you will keep doing to get back at them. If you keep this up you may start getting a sense of the cost of the illusory benefit. Notice how you are feeling in your body as you keep up this attitude.

5. Choose another intention

Now choose a new intention or action. If you have done this process fully and deeply enough, this will usually be forthcoming out of a strong desire to clear things up and make a new start. You may even wish to share your forgiveness in person.

Summary

Look carefully at your ill-will and get out of blame, this process is about *you*, not them.

What have *you* been doing over time to the other person? Own your behaviour.

An attitude has 'stroked' you over the years enabling you to stay in resentment. What is this behaviour which delivers this 'payoff'?

What has it done to your wellbeing over the years? What has it 'cost' you by keeping this pain alive?

Will you offer and receive forgiveness?

What do you choose now to do?

A note about revenge

'We grasp the blade of our revenge with the handle of a justifiable resentment, so we don't notice the blood on our hands.'

- Dr K Bradford Brown

Out of burning resentment comes revenge. Are you caught in this? The dream of triumph, scoring and getting even?

How are you playing it? Have you become a

fishwife, yelling, threatening, insulting and throwing items, or are you on slow burn, plotting and planning? I know of people who let down tyres, removed car batteries, smashed precious collections, or phoned New York and then left the phone off the hook. I have read of the wife who distributed her husband's wine cellar among her neighbours, leaving them like milk bottles on doorsteps, and the wife who cut off one sleeve of each of her husband's tailored suits.

The gain from doing this is power, uplift, high, fun, even laughter; you get to be 'up' while they are 'down' – they got their just deserts and you can be superior, righteous and triumphant.

The truth is that this triumph does not last, it is a momentary gain, which on reflection you will not be proud of. It is easy to hurt someone you know well because you know his or her vulnerable points.

This particular seething, broiling resentment which turns into hatred we call a 'hot' resentment. When you are having difficulty finding anything about this person to like or forgive.

If you are caught in these sorts of behaviour, take a breath and ask yourself 'will the best for all occur if I do this?' If your honest answer is 'no' then it is another opportunity for you to do the Cost Process above and enable yourself to let go of the need for revenge.

***

> **It is easy to hurt someone you know well because you know his or her vulnerable points.**

Guilt

For those of you who have done the leaving you may be feeling a sense of profound relief. This is often followed by guilt. Guilt is not an emotion. It is your mind accusing you of what you have done and how you did it. Guilt, which can be so debilitating if wallowed in, is best handled by verification (see chapter Disease versus Dis-ease). If you did the best you could, with what you had, at the time, forgive yourself and move on. If you know you did not handle it well and you could have done better remember that true shame and remorse are emotions, and feeling them may guide you to offer an apology.

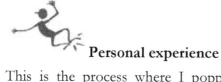

Personal experience

This is the process where I popped out of my socks during my More to Life Weekend. This is the process where I learnt I was a monumental martyr, and I loathe martyrs! Indeed, I am not a martyr about little things but I was failing to *SEE* what a big one I had become. This is the process in which I discovered the payoff and cost of my own controlling behaviours. This is the process that shifted my whole relationship, and gave us the means to communicate for twelve more years. I say 'us' because I am fortunate in that my husband had also taken the More to Life Weekend self-development course so we were speaking the same language.

I have used this process over and over again, whenever resentment comes up. The wonder of it is that you do not have to have the very person sitting in front of you, you merely *imagine* them there, and thus you can do it even if the person has died. If you work deeply your forgiveness will come forward and you can let the years of hate go, and you can forgive them.

14. Completion

"I'm sorry," said often, easily, and without tears, is a sure sign that we will do the same thing again soon.'

- K Bradford Brown

This is a very important part of your separation: the completion of your time and life together. It is the part after which you will be able to move on. In the loss stages you can move on to acceptance, the acceptance that 'it is as it is' which will help you with those recurring questions of 'why me?' It is time to let the past go, notice the lessons you learned, and start your new life.

***

> **It is time to let the past go, notice the lessons you learned, and start your new life.**

I found I needed this part very badly. Having left home and already begun a separate way of living, it seemed too cold, too abrupt to never have a fitting closing. I rang friends, read books and put together a ceremony with bits from everywhere. I share it with you below. We managed to surmount our discord and do this together. If this is impossible for you, please do it on your own. You are of course free to make up your own ceremony, do whatever fits for you both. If your mind is saying, "Oh he/she will never do that," ask them. As Susan Jeffers says, "Feel the fear and do it anyway!" Do not spring it on the other: discuss it, give time to think about it, and pay attention to what each of you would like to do.

You may find the other has a yearning to do something but couldn't quite find what, and is pleased you have come up with something. Maybe you want to go back to a favourite restaurant together, share some wine, and go for a beautiful walk. However you do it I suggest you complete with something, and preferably not in a public place because you will want the freedom to cry.

 Personal experience

Here's what we did. Our house was sold and empty, but the entry date had not yet been reached so it hadn't been moved into by the purchasers. It was a good neutral place to go. Some of the ideas and steps in this ceremony were suggested to me by my friend Clare Vivian-Neal.

COMPLETION CEREMONY

'It is all as simple and as hard as this.'

- K Bradford Brown

We sat opposite each other, either side of an upturned box. On the box was a lit candle and a rose which I cut from the bush in the garden called Wedding Anniversary.

We took turns to speak of what our time together has meant to us, lighting candles for significant times. We lit candles to each of our children, including the son I miscarried.

We said how grateful we were for the many gifts and learnings we have given to and received from each other. This included our various homes and many moves, our joint learnings from taking More to Life, teaching together, the physical side of our relationship, etc.

I acknowledged the failure of my ability to live out my marriage vows 'till death do us part.'

I then cut a white ribbon to break connection between us (I used a ribbon because I went down the aisle with a white ribbon threaded through a prayer book, not a bouquet). I asked my husband to remove my wedding ring and I threaded it onto half of the ribbon. He produced his ring and threaded it onto the other half of the ribbon.

We then agreed the following between us:

We will maintain goodwill for each other and love and honour each other throughout the rest of our lives.

Together, we will love and support our children and grandchildren. We will continue our relationship with them both jointly and separately, upholding each other in our ongoing parenting role.

We will uphold and support each other in our growth, well-being and whatever new relationship we make as we pursue our separate lives.

We will come to each other's assistance in times of need.

We will encourage and respect each other's growth, respective spiritual paths and, our hard work to find reconciliation of our differences.

Let us go forth from this moment in courage and strength.

We exchanged gifts. I received a card with a Celtic blessing, and a dozen red roses. I gave and played the tape of Sarah Brightman and Andrea Borcelli singing 'Time to say goodbye'.

We wept.

'Nothing is ever final, and nothing is ever finished. Every ending is always a new beginning. We are safe. It's only change.'

- Louise Hay

15. Your Will

'The real losers are those who measure their worth by number.'

- K Bradford Brown

Have you made a will?

Have you been meaning to and never got on with it? Do you have a very old one forgotten at the bottom of a drawer? This is not the time to be superstitious and believe you are courting disaster. It is a wise thing to do, and it is quite unnecessary to die intestate. You are in changed circumstances now, and this is the perfect time to make a will.

I would like you to consider making this document, listening to that best side of you, your higher self. Do *not* create anything that will hurt when you have gone. Do not apportion goods from a space of revenge, hate and resentment. You cannot take anything with you when you die, so how about leaving some good?

***

> **Do not apportion goods from a space of revenge, hate and resentment.**

In your life so far, have you longed to inherit some money? Don't you wish Great Auntie Molly had left you something towards a down payment on your first house, a dollop for school fees, or even that gorgeous valuable walnut bureau so that you could get rid of the pine one? Are you in resentment that someone else got the bureau?

It is true that you will have different loyalties now. One or both of you may have a new partner, stepchildren or even more children of your own. To live requires a roof over your head, food to eat, and money, so wouldn't you like to inherit some?

Have you been on the receiving end of a malicious will? Do you know someone who has been? What are your judgments on the deceased? Do you want to be remembered like that?

What your will is for

Your will is about leaving clear instructions for your estate when you die. It is not about parting with anything now. What you do have now is the opportunity to be generous and surprise someone. Most of all surprise your ex-partner. Could your will be a 'thank you' for the home you created together, for the children you had, and for some of the fun? It is so sad to think that from the grave you can have a final stab at hurting someone because you made your will from your place of hurt now.

***

> **What you do have now is the opportunity to be generous and surprise someone.**

If the idea of such generosity is beyond your heart just now, do consider it again later. When your life has settled down and you can call yourself happy once more, it is entirely within your capabilities to add a codicil or simply change your will. Leave something better than you found it.

You have free will.

Some Suggestions for You

Have you considered appointing Guardians for your children? Ideally both parents should agree who, but you may have been left high and dry and now have to choose the person alone.

Firstly, this is not a responsibility to be taken lightly. Guardianship means that when you die they will take your place. This means they will be rearing your children as their own, educating them, influencing them (maybe a different religion), and being their role models. Who will you choose for this role? Some people can leave money for this, and if you cannot you may be placing too big a burden on the surrogate family. Discuss this openly with them and leave them a way out if they cannot take it on.

Also consider that your children need different

things at different ages. Who you appoint when they are toddlers may change when they are teenagers. You can change your will but do remember to tell the guardians what you have done.

Secondly, is your best friend the best person for the job? Will they be a best friend in ten years? Do you admire and like some of their traits but disapprove of others? List all the likely candidates and the pluses. Now make a list of all your reservations, your 'yes buts'.

It may be that you are happy with the godparents you have chosen, or that between your families you are happy with who would come forward. Do remember that, if you appoint Guardians, the children will pass out of the family. Your brothers and sisters will have no future say in anything pertaining to that child. Do you really mean to do this?

Thirdly, do not assume that your parents can have a say. Legally in law, grandparents have no power to change, alter, interfere, rescue or be considered. In your new circumstances the grandparents may be playing a big role in your children's lives. They are loved and you approve of their influence. However, imagine you should die; your partner comes and claims the children and the grandparents on your side will be powerless to change it. The children can be removed to their new home, even a new country, and never see these grandparents again. They simply do not count in law. (Contact rights or Residents rights could be applied for in Scotland.)

Furthermore, if you have named your children in your will, do remember to update it for new babies. If your will is forgotten about and you have failed to add any new children by name (especially if they are grandchildren) they will be left out of inheritance. This can be bewildering and distressing for them, when they know they have been equally loved.

You can see from the above that this whole area of your children's wellbeing needs to be discussed with your partner, so do not dilly-dally!

Note

DIY Will packs from stationers are sufficient for small, uncomplicated estates. For the UK I recommend the *Which? Guide to Giving and Inheriting* by Jonquil Lowe. This book gives tax-efficient ways to pass on money, property and other valuables, and is well worth reading before you consult a solicitor.

16. Remaining Talking versus Remaining Friends

Since the scientists tell us that being 'in love' lasts thirty months, you are unlikely to be still in this state, and at this stage you may have come to realise that this union was all a mistake. Alternatively, your partnership may have become something profound, deep, meaningful and worth every bit of the downs. You may have become 'best friends', but I reckon, if you have, you will still be together.

So the object of this book is to have you remain talking to your partner during and after your separation. If you remain friends, that is a bonus.

Remaining friends

I consider some of the following ingredients make up friendship.

Loyalty to another

This can be found inside and outside families. Men are fantastically loyal to friends, as we know from many a heroic war deed. They are also loyal in often not discussing partner problems with others, whereas women need to talk and confide about it. Men consider this disloyalty and use such phrases as 'she stabbed me in the back'.

One kind of loyalty I find misplaced is that which involves a denial of something patently obvious to everyone – for instance, if the statement, "Your sister is fat, or giggly, or poor at map reading," were hotly denied and the sister defended beyond reasonable explanation. People who indulge in this may find it clouds a friendship because folk are unwilling to tiptoe around you.

Respect

How about your respect for your partner? Is this still intact? In relationship breakdowns one of the first pieces to go is respect. Are you disdainful? Do you consider the other a fool?

Common interests and compatibility

Are you both still interested in the same things? Perhaps your common interests are no longer the same. We have different interests and different friends at different times. Your best buddy from college may not be someone you know now. The best friend you gossiped with about boys became a career girl and is not interested in baby and school talk.

Perhaps your partner pursues a sport or hobby you have no interest in. The problem is, within a relationship there is the expectation that you will both enjoy everything you each do and glow with interest about each other's passion. This may be so when you start off together, but resentment abounds after many years of being left behind the other's dominant interest.

***

> **The problem is that within a relationship, there is the expectation that you will both enjoy everything you each do.**

Compatibility is also about personality. Your personal growth curve will happen at different times to each other; have you been patient and understanding or are you exasperated by a ball and chain? Who we were at twenty-one is not who we are now. People expand or shrink or do not move at all, and problems arise when one person will not accommodate this growth in the other.

Compassion

One of the finest attributes of friendship is compassion – the ability to tolerate our idiosyncrasies, not condone or judge but to love one another for who we are, with the ability to listen well and tell us home truths in a manner which we can hear. It is so helpful in remaining talking to be understanding, empathic and forgiving of our slip-ups. As Jonathan Cainer writes in the *Daily Mail,* 'Compassion requires a particular frame of mind. It is something that has to be reached for, nurtured and developed. A certain amount comes naturally. If you want to manifest more than that, you have to make an effort. The really tricky task is to take two apparently opposing principles (like the need to be kind and the need to be strong) and balance them well.'

Remaining talking

It is more than likely, however, that you may be hurting, bruised, resentful, fearful and angry. You may be thinking that you hope never ever to have contact again, and believe you can wave goodbye without a backward glance. I doubt it.

If this is the case, you might ask yourself what would be your purpose in *not* speaking? Are you out to punish (revenge is sweet)? To diminish the other by imagining yourself superior and above them? Or are you getting some sort of inner glory being a martyr? Or sympathy by being a victim? Are you loading on the guilt, to get rid of your own part of the breakdown? What do you get by *not* speaking?

***

> **It is key in remaining talking to be understanding, empathic and forgiving of our slip-ups.**

If you have children you will need to speak together for all sorts of reasons. You will have situations, school events, visits, etc., to be discussed. If a child gets sick you may have life-saving decisions to be made together. How could any of this be achieved without talking?

To Love, Like, Hate or…

If your relationship has none of the listed ingredients above then you are not friends and can't pretend to be, so the best you can aim for is to stay talking.

Staying talking is in a sense staying friends, but the boundaries have changed.

It *is* possible to honour, respect and love your partner as a fellow human being. They are on their life's journey, and much as you may wish to change them they are as they are.

***

In friendship we seek out the other in order to share and be of support.

At a wedding recently the vicar stood up to give his address and his opening words were: "Do you know what the bride's first three encounters are at the church? They are aisle, altar, hymn. Translated, this is I'll alter him!" This vicar continued with such an amusing, enlightened, and passionate talk that he must have been experiencing trying to be changed himself. Why do women want to change men? How come they cannot resist or desist trying it? Did you embark on this relationship happy with who you found or did you harbour dreams of changing the other from the start?

…Indifference

The opposite to love is not hate – you can get

passionate about both. The opposite to love is indifference. If you are indifferent to your partner then I believe you no longer love them. In fact, you probably don't even like them and in this case you do not even have a basis of friendship either. The best you can aim for is to stay talking.

Personal experience

When I married at nineteen I thought the sun shone out of my husband. I took his opinions as my own and hung on his every word. Our interests were, I now know, very different, but on my wedding day I was willing to take up, explore and learn anything that came my way.

I did not, however, embrace his religion and our early years were spent with him desperately trying to convert me and me yelling that he could believe what he liked but that he shouldn't impose it on me. Spiritually, we were miles apart.

However, afraid of authority and bullies, I did not assert myself until well into my thirties. Sadly, having already set up the pattern of power play, roles, expectations, etc. any change of my behaviour brought on a parent-like dominance from my husband. I would go into 'pleasing child' behaviours to keep the peace. Thus, seething with resentment, I enabled us to play out roles I did not want nor agreed with.

By my forties, we were searching for help and got into 'self-development'. I took to it like a duck to water and sponged up as much as I could learn and use. I am pragmatic and I am good at converting what I learn intellectually into changing my way of thinking and my actions. I will and do give it a try. But catching and *changing* our automaticity or habits and actually *doing* something differently is a big challenge. I think the phrase is, 'don't just talk the talk, but walk the walk'. Theory is no good if not practiced.

Aged fifty I had learned that I am who I am. I have done the best I could with what I had at the time. I aim to leave something better than I found it, and if this book enables you to leave your relationship in such a manner that you can forgive yourself and your partner, remain talking without any underlying current of resentment, then I salute myself and you for a job well done.

17. Falling in Love Again…

Since writing my suspicions of what happens when we fall 'in love' in the chapter titled 'Results of Separation', I have read an article in a past issue of *LIFE* called 'The Science of Love', by Nuna Alberts. This article translates my guesses into chemical findings. Researchers have discovered that romance, quite literally, requires certain chemistry. The writer Nuna Alberts reports that researchers now know why one glimpse of the right person can set off a chemical reaction leading to romance.

But what happens after that? Why do some relationships succeed while others fizzle out? We know that traits from scent to facial symmetry determine your appeal, but what happens in the body? Here is a shortened extract from the article:

When a man goes to a party the first step, while scanning a room, is unconscious noting of facial symmetry, then body shape and finally eye contact. If she smiles his midbrain - the part that controls visual and auditory reflexes - releases the neurotransmitter dopamine, a brain chemical that gives him a rush and the motivation to initiate conversation. As he nears, his pheromones reach

her hypothalamus, eliciting a 'Yes, come closer,' look. He is now feeling the first flutter of sexual attraction. His hypothalamus, the brain region that is responsible for emotions, tells his body to send out attraction signals. He gets her phone number.

The next day, memories of this contact direct his brain to secrete increasing levels of dopamine giving strong feelings of pleasure. When they meet the next night his stomach does flip-flops and he starts feeling giddy at the sight of her. He can think of nothing but that face, those eyes, that smile, as his brain pathways become intoxicated with elevated levels of dopamine, norepinephrine (another neurotransmitter) and, particularly, phenylethylamine (PEA). This cocktail of natural chemicals gives him a slight buzz and contributes to the almost irrational feelings of attraction - which we've all felt - that begin dominating his thoughts at work, while driving, as he goes to sleep. It's a natural high. In the weeks that follow the relationship deepens. The first night of bringing her home his body floods with the chemical oxytocin; so does hers and the couple start forming a bond. Scientists now think that oxytocin actually strengthens the brain's receptors that produce emotions. Oxytocin increases further with touching, cuddling and other stages of intimacy. It may also make it easier to evoke pleasant memories of each other while apart. Next comes the wedding. Honeymoon. Now what?

Fast-forward 18 months. At this point the couple could be at a crossroads. Science tells us that 18 months to three years after the first moment of infatuation, it's not unusual for feelings of neutrality for one's love partner to set in. For many there could be a chemical explanation. The mix of dopamine, norepinephrine and PEA is so much like a drug, say scientists, that it takes greater and greater doses to get the same buzz. So after someone has been with one person for a time, his brain stops reacting to the chemicals because it is habituated. 'The brain can't maintain the revved-up status,' says Anthony Walsh, professor of criminology at Boise State University and author of *The Science of Love: Understanding Love and Its Effects on Mind and Body*. 'As happens with any drug, it needs more and more PEA to make the heart go pitter-patter.' Couples with attachments that are shaky for other reasons (money woes, abuse, irreconcilable differences) may part and - because the body's tolerance of PEA soon diminishes- seek someone new with whom to find the thrill of early love.

More likely, however, committed couples will move on to what science suggests is the most rewarding and enduring aspect of love. Though the same addictive rush isn't involved, ongoing physical contact, not just sex, helps produce endorphins, another brain chemical, and high doses of oxytocin.

Well, now you know what may have been behind the dying embers of your romance, partnership or marriage, and why an affair began or indeed why it ended. The point is that knowing this you can be knowledgeable about your next in-love relationship. You can enjoy the buzz again and at the same time be wise about the outcome and therefore make an informed decision about remarriage.

18. … And Getting Remarried

'Need is the thing that holds a marriage together over the long haul. If the need stops, the marriage stops.'

- Carroll O'Connor

Some of you will, some of you won't. Some of you may be longing for companionship, security, love, physical touch, children, etc. Others of you may have a high fence around you with 'keep out' notices!

Back-chat and discussions often reveal the dismay that a mutual friend has repeated a pattern and married the same type! Why does this happen? I have a theory that if the remarriage is quick you will be attracted to the same type of person. You still have growth to achieve. This person is likely to be the same as or the opposite of a parent. They were our role models and we learnt how to play our parts alongside them as small children. If time elapses before the next marriage you are likely to have made changes to yourself, and may know what you do and don't find acceptable in another. You're all set to choose a totally different type. Often these marriages work and are extremely happy.

The chances of getting back together

So you haven't yet found a totally different type of partner and now dwell on the possibility of getting back together. Distance has erased some of your difficulties and you remember with fondness the partner you had; you are sure you have both changed enough to try again.

The point is, yes, you both may have changed, but have you continued to work on your differences *together* at all? Have you been able to discuss what went wrong? Have you, with time, been able to own your part in the break-up, and notice what you did and why?

It takes two to 'crazy-make'; each of you will have participated, and even if you blame the other for 'always' reacting in such and such a manner, you yourself will have behaved in a way which enables the other to slip into their automaticity.

I do recommend an enlightening little book by Dr George R Bach and Ronald M Deutsch called *Stop! You're Driving Me Crazy*. In it he says:

Typical crazymaking by intimates is rarely what it appears to be – a strangely maddening annoyance born of seeming carelessness, forgetfulness, or accident. Instead, it is usually an urgent message about a concealed problem, a problem that is central to the relationship. But it is a message in code.

Unless we can read that code, we cannot recognise the problem or deal with it. The result is that the crazymaking will continue to recur. And as it recurs, it will steadily erode the

relationship. It can destroy the trust and goodwill we need with lovers and co-workers, with parents and children.

It is no good assuming that distance and time have changed the crazymaking patterns you developed together. It's true, you probably do not do the same things with another but then, nor do they. For any hope of getting back together you will both need to explore what previously set you both off, and then encourage each other to do things differently.

Likewise, you may need to look at the power struggle that went on between you both. Perhaps this need to control was the cause of your parting? As I tried to stay in my marriage I read countless books and each made sense to me at the time. They seemed to say so eloquently what I had suspected was happening but could not find words with which to express myself or make sense. For this reason I include quotes, where appropriate, in the hope that if something also makes sense to you it will be of some help.

Power struggle and control were definitely instrumental in our separation. Two 'Top Dog' characters, we vied for position as king of the castle. This is an explosive mixture if the position-sharing becomes unbalanced and the underdog of the moment doesn't get their turn to shine.

Difficult interactions will typically have us take a stance from the three dispositions of Persecutor, Rescuer or Victim. At any time we can and do move around these roles. The problems start when positions become so entrenched that you can't get out and the power struggle turns into a constant conflict. It's exhausting to live in and unpleasant for others to be around.

The trick is to power-share without one partner believing they are inadequate or threatened if it is not their turn. This means having genuine self-esteem in place, coupled with humility. Our personal growth requires both sides of the master/servant role to be experienced just as we are both teacher and pupil throughout our lives.

Now, you are out of the relationship with thoughts of returning to it – how will this power base have changed? In *Do I Have to Give Up Me to be Loved by You?* Drs Jordan and Margaret Paul suggest that:

Sometimes power struggles so pervade a couple's interactions that even trivial issues turn into a hot or cold war. When two people become entrenched in their respective positions, a separation is sometimes the only way for them to obtain a different perspective on their problems. When couples separate and *continue to work on their relationship* – each understanding his or her part of the power struggle – they usually resolve their problems and eventually get back together.

Separation *without insight* into power struggles usually does not break them. Some couples separate, eventually divorce, and years later are still locked in power struggles. Other couples feel wonderful towards each other while separated – feeling alive and sexual in ways they had not felt since the beginning of their

relationship – only to fall back into their old patterns when they move back together.

The request that initiates a power struggle is often reasonable, and your partner's refusal may make no sense to you. You may then attempt to explain logically why you feel as you do and want what you want. Your partner's continuing resistance may then bring out your heavy artillery – threats, crying, yelling. But nothing works. You become increasingly frustrated, hurt and angry. You feel unloved. What's your option? Keep trying? Give up? Neither will work, unfortunately. You can't give up wanting what you want and to keep trying entrenches your partner in resisting; and the distance increases. The solution comes with an intent to learn.

Breaking power struggles is very difficult because they are often subtle and reactions have become automatic: You want, he or she resists, you pull harder, etc. But it's one thing to want your partner to be different and another thing to try to make him or her change. There is only one way that change comes about without creating a power struggle – to continue to want what you want, but when you don't get it, explore why not.

So what are the common pinch-points, power struggles and crazymaking patterns of a relationship which recur and recur? In the 1980s the divorce rate soared and our local Relate (Marriage Guidance Council) happened to have counsellors who were Catholic. Having discovered that there are four common areas of discord they suggested a scheme called 'Link Couples' to the Cambridge Monseigneur who adopted it in his diocese. Boldly, this church decided to confront these four areas, namely, Money, Roles, Sex and Spirituality, before a couple went down the aisle. To do this they requested couples who had been married for a minimum of five years to come forward and be willing to explore and talk through these areas with engaged couples. We took part in this and it was a fascinating experience. It never ceased to amaze us how little pre-marriage discussion had gone on regarding major decisions. The couple were often focused on the actual wedding day, frequently duelling over whether the cake should be round or square, for instance, and disregarding bigger topics.

Budget and accounting

Some questions to address are:

· Whose money is it?

· Do you consider your earnings as yours and your partner's earnings as joint?

· Will you have a joint account?

· Do you fall into the trap of believing your partner does not trust you or love you if you do not want a joint account?

· If you have a joint account, what agreements will you have that one partner does not empty it on purchasing a motorbike while you had your eye on carpeting the bedroom?

· If you are both earning, when you marry will it

all go into one pot or will you want to keep an account for yourself?

· If you have been an earner and then stop work how will you handle expenses?

· How will it be not to 'have your own money'?

· What about credit cards? (One of you may believe they are dangerous and refuse to have one, while the other may consider them a way of life and wouldn't be without one.) How about hire-purchase or store cards which enable you to pay off slowly?

***

> **Both parties will come to the union with expectations of how it will be and it is a big shock to find that your two maps do not match.**

Roles and expectations

What baggage have you brought to this partnership about male and female roles in the home? This will also have been determined by how your parents did it. If he sees himself as 'hunter gatherer', do you do the opposite? Or are you also a hunter and a gatherer and very capable too? In which case how are the domestic chores worked out?

Will you divide into roles of 'manly' work like car maintenance, logs and fire lighting, and money matters for him, and washing, ironing etc. for her? In which case, who changes a fuse and who carves the joint of meat?

Unfortunately men fail to realize that women do

all these jobs when they are away. Sadly, for the sake of peace, women often downplay their capabilities and perform 'little girl' in order for the manly pride not to be piqued – that she can do many things not only well but better!

What about quarrels in your own home? Did your parents let rip or was there tense silence for days? How did things get sorted or made up? Tears and a kiss, or sliding back into communication but still treading on eggshells? It is a shock for a couple to find their first little row becoming a mega-meltdown because of different expectations.

***

> **It is a shock for a couple to find their first little row becoming a mega-meltdown because of different expectations.**

If your partner has never had the freedom to speak their mind, their silence may wind you up because you prefer to have a good yell and then it is over. In these cases, the initial reason for the row is usually forgotten and the focus now is on how he/she does or doesn't row! There is then a make wrong time because your way is right and theirs is wrong… and three months after the wedding you believe getting married was a mistake!

Sex and sexuality

If you are in the flush of a physical union which is

the best ever and which surely will remain like this, you might like to consider what – other than gymnastics – might sex contribute to the marriage? When the incredible physical attraction abates you will be left with a partner who is ordinary, and lovemaking will slide into companionship, trust, love, hope, and saying sorry. I would not include reconciliation. In my own experience, if lovemaking is used to patch up a quarrel or used to end a dispute, it is extremely hard to bring up the topic again. This may leave things unresolved and festering. It seems women need to be reconciled to enjoy the act whereas men may use the act as reconciliation and then believe all is well.

***

It seems women need to be reconciled to enjoy sex whereas men may use sex as reconciliation and then believe all is well.

John Gottman in *Why Marriages Succeed or Fail* says about men: "There are often no emotional prerequisites for having sex because closeness is the goal, not the cause, of a sex act thus men can have sex even if they are feeling distant, argumentative, or angry," whereas for most women, "Making love confirms intimacy rather than creates it."

Spirituality

Do you think alike about G.O.D., whoever or whatever this may be? Are you convinced you are soul mates and are practically telepathic, or are you in awed respect of the other's convictions? Marrying into a different religion, belief system or philosophy can be a minefield of misunderstandings. Have you talked about them? Are you in agreement about what you will teach your children?

We are often extremely ignorant of another country's culture. We may be in the European Union but there is a world of difference marrying into an Italian, Greek or French family. You are free to choose what you do, but remember that others who love you are also going to be affected by your decisions, even more so if you marry into the customs of the Middle East or Asia.

With these areas highlighted and discussed you have a good chance of making a wonderful, fulfilling next union.

19. Results of Separation

Where am I now?

'That you gifted me with love once does not mean you owe it to me today.'

- K Bradford Brown

I have let go of any regrets. Only now, in the knowledge of experience of living alone and enjoying it, secure in finance, can I honestly even consider regret that I stayed so long and did not do something about my discontent earlier.

I trust the timing completely. Deep inside I know I could not have gone earlier, as the timing was not right. When I tried I was stopped by other monumental, unanticipated events. I also know that I was not strong enough, brave enough, or secure enough.

I do regret that I didn't live out my marriage vows. I adored my husband when I married him and I had every intention of marrying for life.

Finance

This scared me silly. As I've already said, I was a 'kept woman' with few trained qualifications, and making my own way at fifty seemed impossible. However, here I am flourishing. As a natural born speculator married to a hoarder, I never could amass enough finance of my own with which to create more. Now I have a finger in many pies, and all are making money. I am not living frugally and in fear. I am using what I have to make more, trusting I shall, and loving every minute of it!

Relationships

I cannot imagine marrying again. I do not want to slip into my role of wifely deferral, compliance and then resent another's demands. I believe I would suppress my needs and lose my new found 'Self'. It would have to be a very extraordinary man because our age group does not live with the same freedoms of the next generation. We were reared by parents fresh out of the Victorian era, and male and female roles were culturally defined. The wife stayed at home with no expectation of working, her contribution was homemaking, child-rearing and some unthreatening hobbies to keep her occupied. The husband, the main earner, handled all the finances of home and holidays. Anyone wanting to take up with me, by dint of age, comes from this background. I can, however, imagine an arms-length relationship. This would look like regular visits, sharing and enjoying, but not living together.

What I frequently see with couples, especially young ones, is a rushing to the altar on the 'in love' high. This can and does become a bedrock of love and lasts, or it fizzles out and breaks up. The falsity of this 'in love' period deceives you into seeing the other's traits and habits as endearing, and you have a high tolerance level of whims, peculiarities and behaviours. I notice that when this wears off the tolerance level drops, and these same traits now irritate. Communication breaks down, quarrels abound. What the other does now is 'wrong' and you are 'right' – why can't they change? – HA!

Good luck. You will do better by changing yourself. There is no doubt that when you break the Ping-Pong pattern and *you* do something differently, then *they* will too. You have broken the chain of inevitability about where this argument will go. But this takes hard work, and the truth is I am out of 'try'. The idea of returning to constantly adjusting, the daily compromises, the effort it takes to 'read' the other and tiptoeing around moods, frankly exhausts me to think about it.

Health

I was thin to start with and lost a further 1.5 stone (21 lb.) over the separation. If I do wake in the night I now go back to sleep instead of remaining wide-eyed with my brain working overtime. What has gone is the awful three-day stomach cramps. During the latter years of our marriage each contretemps or row would have me doubled up. Once, when the pain was continuous, I went through all the ulcer investigations.

It is all nerves. Our delicate, finely tuned nervous system will lodge its dis-ease somewhere in each of us, as constipation, diarrhoea, migraine, eczema, nausea, etc. Mine shows up in my stomach with grinding cramps which take three days to work down from under the ribcage, to belly, to bowel. Even after I had left home after each visit or meeting with lawyers, the cramps would come back. Do your best at self-help, knowing that it is in your mind and that 'this too will pass.'

I do still have frightening dreams. After any contact I have a dream from which I wake with a pounding heart. The dream is always about being controlled, rowing about it, and then being afraid. I do not know if this subconscious repetition is reminding me I am now free, or if I still need to rid myself of a lot of angst.

Growth area

There is no doubt in my mind that this separation needed to happen. You can blow on the embers of a marriage and rekindle it, but without cherishing the flame it will diminish again. We had ceased to grow – in fact we were stunting each other. I believe that our individual growth will now gallop away. To begin with, I have come out from behind 'Daddy' and I believe my husband has let 'Mummy' go. It was time.

Loss

This may be hard to fathom, since I wanted and instigated the separation, but I do have a sense of loss. I, who was so afraid of losing him, controlled him over women. If I lost him I was a failure, and now here I am making him available. I, who cannot lose a biro, sack anyone or put my ailing animals down, have created this big loss in my life. My stories and reminiscences are still about my married life – how could they not be? Until new experiences give me a file, nostalgia and our history are what I have to draw on.

I am in a push-me pull-me of emotions. One minute I want to share something and mentally write an email, the next I resist because that does not help either of us separate. I come into an answerphone message from him and I feel invaded, the next I know I do not want to totally sever contact. Recently, I wandered into a gallery and saw the most stunning small sculpture (called 'Sunday Morning') of a naked couple shamelessly lying in a 'spoons' position. As we liked to do this I immediately wanted to contact him about it – what for?

There is no question I wish him well, want him to be happy, and of course have a relationship if he wants one, *and* there will be a tug when he does. I let him go with love.

Children

We are in regular contact and I see them. I do not believe any of them has taken sides and I do not feel judged by them. I think they have gone through this magnificently and I am proud of them and proud of how we managed it.

I have had comments of, "You are both very different people now", "You are the most relaxed I've seen you in ages", "It's important you are happy". But that is all I hear.

Separation

Whether you have been painfully left or done the leaving, this is *your* life's journey and what *you* make of it. Your level of resistance to change will be the measure of how quickly you pick yourself up again. The choice is yours. Will you remain bitter, resentful and fearful of any future relationship? Or will you bounce and be that free spirit you are and which will attract another if that is what you want? Who wants to live with a self-righteous misery?!

 **Post script**

Since writing this chapter my husband has phoned to say he has met someone. Emotions simply do not follow the logic – that I instigated and wanted this separation. I feel empty in the stomach - she has what I want, a relationship with a fine man, but from a distance so the tolerance level remains high. Mrs Stephens, who wants her family, home and marriage is jealous. Gilli does not envy her. No matter how bitter your parting, and whether you have forgiven your partner, I do not believe that you will not be moved when they find another.

'In marriage we become partners for life in more ways than one. Those invisible bonds are seldom severed for any reason, including divorce.'

- K Bradford Brown

20. Self-Help

'No matter how much you protest, you are totally responsible for everything that happens in your life.'

- Wayne Dyer

This book is not intended to be a self-development book. It is manual to guide you through some of the painful passages and pitfalls. I have drawn on the many books I have read and the courses I have taken. The list below has the ones from which I gleaned the most, the ones where I got a nugget that I could instantly implement and change something for myself.

It is easy to spot our other half's dramas and behaviours, and less easy to notice our own. Notice your resistance either to reading something or to taking a course. What are the reasons you give? My guess is that behind such reasons as lack of time and money there is fear. Fear of exposure, fear of finding out something you don't like, fear that you are not perfect. Rest assured you are worthy just as you are *and* you may be doing some things which do not serve you and which you can change.

If your reasons for not exploring yourself are along the lines of 'it's American', or even a fear of being 'sucked in' or 'taken over' by a cult remind yourself that some excellent work, courses and books originated in America and that writing off something because you can blame a nation's navel-gazing is not worthy of you. If you are of a mind to think you do not *need* it, notice the arrogance with which you hold yourself, your superiority over others and the disdain in which you hold others who do this work.

Your marriage has ended; can you look in the mirror and say it was all the other's fault? Look again.

I have mentioned the *More to Life Programme* in several chapters. This programme offers practical skills to enhance your relationships, deepen your self-awareness, and develop your ability to create the results you want in your life, via experiential courses such as Relationships, Sexuality, Parenting, Making Money Count, Opening the Heart, Strengthening the Will and many more. Before any of these focus courses may be taken, you take the More to Life Weekend, an intensive thirty-five hours of experiential learning. This initial weekend is the starter pack where you learn about the value of your word and your authority; the games you play and the 'mindtalk' that runs you.

The bedrock of the programme is the Clearing Process, without which I would stay stuck and below the line daily. You will learn about the handling of resentments with the Cost Process, which I have written about in the chapter on 'Regrets versus Resentments', as well as the disavowal of the lies you have told yourself and the avowal of the truth; and finally you bring yourself home with the 'I Am' process. It is healing and forgiving. It is fast. You will work with others, learn from others, discover you are not alone, and will save yourself hours and weeks with a counsellor. It is the best training I know of.

The More to Life Centres and website www.moretolife.org.uk will inform you of guest events and introductory evenings for you to find out more.

Book List

Anything of John Gray's, especially *Men are from Mars, Women are from Venus, Mars and Venus Together Forever,* and *Mars and Venus in the Bedroom, Starting Over.*

Anything by Harville Hendrix, especially *Getting The Love You Want,* and

Keeping the Love you Find

Stop! You're Driving me Crazy by Dr George R. Bach and Ronald M. Deutsch

Other People's Children by Joanna Trollope

Do I Have to Give Up Me To Be Loved By You by Drs Jordan and Margaret Paul

Why Marriages Succeed or Fail by John Gottman

More to Life Centres are Worldwide

UK
London
North England
Scotland

Germany
Kiel

USA
California, Bay Area
Texas Houston
Huntsville
New York
Montana Bozeman
Minneapolis

New Zealand
Tauranga

Australia
Victoria

South Africa
Johannesburg
Durban
Cape Town

Web Page: http://www.moretolife.org.uk

About the Author

I married just out of my gym slip at the age of nineteen and did not start a career until my children were all in school.

I spent ten years as an Interior Designer and, because I can visualise a finished room, I had a wonderful time doing the show houses for Brosley homes.

We moved south from Scotland and as the marriage cracks were widening we agreed to go to marriage guidance, now called Relate. There was an eight-week wait for a place.

Out of the blue, within those eight weeks, we heard about a self-development training course called More to Life which we thought might help us. My sister, brother-in-law, and my husband took the weekend course while I stayed at home with the children.

On Monday evening my husband walked in looking five years younger and full of interesting information about how we live our lives out of beliefs (many false) about ourselves and others. I was fascinated and had a frustrating six weeks to wait before I could take the next training.

I was hooked. I found the experiential learning and processes appealed to my pragmatic nature. Here was the 'how to' to change what I did that did not serve me. It showed me how I could be happier in my relationship and go forward with new understanding and hope.

I became a teacher of Self Esteem Empowerment, a focus course within the More to Life Programme. I taught privately, in social services, as evening classes in a community college and in Littlehey Prison. I found the work rewarding and enriching because it also taught me listening skills, empathising and a deeper understanding of people's conflicts. In my experience, relationships make the world go round, not money.

We moved back to Scotland. I continued teaching but thought I needed a challenge so I changed tack, created and ran an accommodation agency for the annual festival. With a willing friend we developed Festival Beds which offered B&B in people's city centre homes. It was, and still is, a huge success.

Without children at home to dilute our problems and differences the marriage was floundering. More to Life had given us fifteen more years and had seen the children out; it was time for me to leave.

The result of separating is this book, in which I hope I have passed on some tips, advice and suggestions to help you through your own difficult time.

25537564R00084

Printed in Great Britain
by Amazon